AF271504

ETERNAL AMERICA

It is not the level of prosperity that makes for happiness but the kinship of heart to heart and the way we look at the world ... a man can choose to be happy and no one can stop him—

Yoshikazu Shirakawa

ETERNAL

AMERICA

KODANSHA INTERNATIONAL LTD.
Tokyo, New York & San Francisco

Darkness becomes light . . .

Quotations on page 215 from *The Singing Wilderness* (copyright © 1956 by Sigurd F. Olson) and *Open Horizons* (copyright © 1969 by Sigurd F. Olson) courtesy of Alfred A. Knopf, Inc.

Distributors:

United States: Harper & Row, Publishers, Inc.
 10 East 53rd Street, New York, New York 10022

South America: Harper & Row, International Department

Canada: Fitzhenry & Whiteside Limited
 150 Lesmill Road, Don Mills, Ontario

Mexico & Central America: HARLA S.A. de C.V.
 Apartado 30–546, Mexico 4, D.F.

United Kingdom: TABS
 7 Maiden Lane, London WC2

Europe: Boxerbooks Inc.
 Limmatstrasse 111, 8031 Zurich

Australia & New Zealand: Book Wise (Australia) Pty. Ltd.
 104–8 Sussex Street, Sydney 2000

Thailand: Central Department Store Ltd.
 306 Silom Road, Bangkok

Hong Kong & Singapore: Books for Asia Ltd.
 30 Tat Chee Avenue, Kowloon
 65 Crescent Road, Singapore 15

The Far East: Japan Publications Trading Company
 P.O. Box 5030, Tokyo International, Tokyo

Published by Kodansha International Ltd., 2–12–21 Otowa, Bunkyo-ku, Tokyo 112 and Kodansha International/USA, Ltd., 30 East 53rd Street, New York, New York 10022 and 44 Montgomery Street, San Francisco, California 94104.
Text copyright © 1975 by Kodansha International Ltd. Photographs copyright © 1975 by Yoshikazu Shirakawa.
All rights reserved. Printed in Japan.

LCC 74–29564
ISBN 0–87011–249–x
JBC 0072–784665–2361

First edition, 1975
Third printing, 1975

Contents

Foreword

William O. Douglas

Eternal America is a photographic tribute to our continent. Mountains, rolling plains, high alpine basins, rugged coastlines, great deserts, like men, come and go. By man's clock they are everlasting, yet by the cosmic clock they are fleeting. Beyond each visible scene are views beyond the reach of the camera. Plains and low mountains, now dry and desertic, once dripped with water and grew giant Pleistocene trees, perhaps the Douglas fir. One can occasionally find them in the high basins of our southwest—in the eight-thousand-foot zone. Even desert wastes have underground streams coursing through limestone ledges that are largely uncharted. Great upheavals of rock, molten lava flowing from fissures, vast granite intrusions are the spectacular aspects of planetary forces. Beyond that are minutiae, which collectively make up another wonderland. In the small as in the massive strokes of the sculptor are the unceasing wonders of our earth.

Man occupies but a small percentage of the land. Viewed from the air, the occupied area is only a series of small oases. Rugged canyon walls enclose some, volcanic debris contains others, and scant rainfall puts manifold acres beyond much human use.

Technically the Great American Desert includes not only southern California, Arizona, New Mexico, and West Texas but also western slices of Oklahoma, Kansas, Nebraska, South Dakota, and even part of Colorado, Wyoming, Montana, Idaho, Oregon and Washington. The exact boundary depends on the cycle of rainfall. There is more to the desert than sand. Much of the American desert is composed of rocky plateaus. They are distinguished by low rainfall, high daytime temperature, low nighttime temperature, high winds, a high rate of evaporation and a sparse and scattered plant life. Parts of this vast area are only partially desert and some, part-time deserts, depending on cycles of weather.

Mountains are the main cause of deserts, for they cut off the rain clouds. The mountain ranges responsible for the Great American Desert are the Sierra Nevada and the Rockies, but when most laymen think of the Great American Desert, they think of southern California and southern Arizona, New Mexico, and West Texas. Streams in these areas have headwaters in rainy areas but flow across dry land. The Colorado and Rio Grande are the waterways of our main American desert.

There are places in this desert where man does not flourish, yet other animals do. The kangaroo rat takes over the desert and would be supreme but for the rattlesnake and coyote, which cast the balance and make for stability. The kangaroo rat lines its run-

ways with the cholla cactus to keep coyotes from digging him out. The kangaroo rat
has a unique capacity: it extracts hydrogen and oxygen from its food and makes its own
water, so droughts never bother it. Here too are prairie dogs and a wide variety of
lizards, only two of which are poisonous: the gila monster and the Mexican beaded
lizard. The gila monster seemingly lives in a stupor, which makes it practically harmless
to man, unless one puts his finger in its mouth. In other basins the coyote helps keep
the rabbit and ground squirrel population down. The sharp-shinned hawk is a deadly
killer, making prey even out of the English sparrow that frequents the desert. The
horned owl hunts at night, locating its prey by listening to the small sounds that reflect
the terror of the victims when they hear its hoot—two rapid *hoo-hoos* followed by two
slower ones. On the margin of the desert and leading up into the hills where deer graze
is the cougar, another agent placed by the Creator on our wondrous continent for population control. Here too is the javelina (wild hog or peccary), running in herds.

These deserts of ours that have a quiet majestic look are alive with creatures, playing
specialized roles in the cosmic plan. The roadrunner—a long-legged bird that never
flies—means death to snakes. The valley quail gorges on the abundant seeds and insects
produced by exotic desert flowers, which have fleeting hours of glory before being trans-
formed into coarse pods.

One who tramps the vast expanses has a first impression that they are hostile to man.
Yet if he returns often enough, he learns there are small pockets of water in many
cacti, that many pods are edible, and that dried roots are available for fuel. The most
majestic of the cacti, the saguaro, lives long years by man's calendar. Its fine roots run
close to the surface of the earth and, when great rains come, soak up the water, which
is stored in tubular recesses within the plant for use when the great droughts come.

The desert, rich in the resources that build an interrelated community of flora and
fauna, has spiritual values for man. The bunch grass in these deserts softly sings when
the wind blows, but one has to listen reverently to hear it. As John Muir wrote, "Music
belongs to all matter. There is not a silent, songless particle in the Lord's creation."

The saguaros are almost human in the gestures they make. In the dusk or in the gray-
ness before dawn, a forest of them takes on a weird and ghostly appearance. The trees,
their arms thrown skyward, look like dancers frozen in some weird pantomime. There
may be a dozen or more arms on a single plant. And they may multiply until the tree
is 150 to 200 years old.

Saguaro, in Indian, means friend, and friend it is. Its beautiful, white, nocturnal flowers, which have the fragrance of a ripe melon, produce a figlike, edible fruit. Its seeds
make up into butter. Its wood furnishes shelter and fuel.

The gila woodpecker is partial to the saguaro cactus, drilling its nest there, which, in
time, the tiny elf owl takes over.

The apparent poverty of the desert and its austerity combine to make man contem-
plate the narrow margin between life and destruction.

Out of the desert came great teachers: Jesus and Mohammed, and before them Zoroaster, and much later the Bab. The desert sets man speculating as to the why of life, as well as the whence. Nighttime even increases the intensity of that speculation, for the stars over the desert always seem unusually close and intimate. It is no coincidence that the habitat of the Bedouin became the great celestial observatory.

The American deserts have been put into great jeopardy by man. Mechanized vehicles, known as "dune-buggies," now roar across them, churning the fragile soil and uprooting the sparse vegetation. As population increases, these vehicles, unless restrained, will produce a Sahara-type desert of shifting sands that will eat savagely into its edges, as it moves east and north under the force of winds.

Dune-buggies are not the only destructive force at work. Overgrazing on once lush lands has produced millions of acres in America that are no longer an intact ecological unit. One can measure them by the spread of the mesquite tree. This mesquite, which looks much like a peach orchard when one rides through it, is an important and valuable tree. It has a vast root system that helps hold the soil during flashfloods. Its early twigs are browse for deer and cattle. Its pods were used by the Indians to make flour and mush; cattle love them. They are indeed nutritious, for they contain dextrose. The Indians used its gum for wounds and sores. They also obtained a black dye from it and also used it as a glue. Mesquite bark was useful in tanning and dyeing. Its trunk is valuable for fence posts and for corral stockades. Its wood, particularly the root and underground stems, makes a hot fire that leaves good coals. And the smoke of a mesquite fire is for me filled with so many memories of campfires that it is haunting.

But the mesquite, in spite of its great virtues, brings sad news as well as good. The mesquite seed, traveling through cattle dung, spreads fast. The seeds cannot compete on the range when the sod is good. It can get a foothold only when the range is overgrazed. That is to say, the range is broken down as an ecologic entity before the mesquite starts its migration. Once it starts to march, it becomes the master, for it shades out grass and competes with other plants for moisture. Gradually it takes over.

In our western country the mark of ecological harm is evident on many mountain slopes. As a result of overgrazing by sheep- and cattlemen—a form of subsidy when it is on government land, as it usually is—the bunchgrass and wheatgrass are lost and cheat grass takes over. Cheat grass never forms live sod but only dies and reseeds like crabgrass.

Man's destruction of predators usually has a disastrous impact on the land, for it increases the chances of overgrazing of one or more plants. I related in *Farewell to Texas* the ecologist's view that the poisoning of coyotes and the shooting of golden eagles results in the increasing pressure of sheep on the land. One of the outstanding features of Texas is indeed overgrazing by sheep of the fragile, semidesertic country.

In Arizona the superintendent of the Saguaro National Monument near Tucson in the 1950s undertook the elimination of rattlesnakes. That portion of Arizona has thirteen species of rattlesnakes, and tourists conscious of the danger of exposure to them would not venture into the grounds of the monument. So the superintendent put his staff to work killing rattlesnakes and gave that activity wide publicity. The snakes disappeared and the tourists returned, making the superintendent's reports to Washington, D.C., more interesting, for now the payment of tourist fees mounted, and the appropriation committee in Congress knew that this particular monument was being "successful." Pretty soon, however, the superintendent became worried, for there were no new saguaros sprouting. He sounded the alarm, and Washington sent out a scientist, who was a friend of mine. The scientist discovered that the saguaros were not sprouting because with the demise of the snakes, the kangaroo rat population had exploded, and those rats were eating the tender sprouts of the new saguaro. The remedy adopted by the superintendent was not readmittance of the snakes but the construction of a greenhouse where saguaros were grown until they passed through this tender sprout stage and became unattractive to rodents.

Man's war on the coyote in the mountainous John Day area of southeast Oregon was so severe that the deer population exploded. The number of deer so exceeded the supply of food on the ranges that they died like flies in the wintertime.

The phenomenon is not peculiar to the land; it is repeated in offshore waters. The kelp found both in the Pacific and Atlantic off our coasts is a mainstay of ocean life, just as bunchgrass is in the Great Plains. The main types are *Laminaria* and *Agarium*. Sea urchins unless restrained overpopulate the coastal zones and the health of the kelp suffers. Lobster are a main predator of sea urchins, but man's search for the delicacies of lobster meat has endangered the lobster. As the lobster population has dropped, the sea urchin population has mounted with the consequent depletion of kelp.

So, whether we look to the deserts, to the plains, or to the mountains, or to the ocean, nature's balance, provided by predators, is often upset by man with tragic consequences.

The mark of glaciers is on the northern sectors of our land. Basins survived in New York, Michigan, Wisconsin and Minnesota, becoming in time lakes rich in nutrients and sustaining much fish and birdlife. Glacial moraines worked their southward movement; the one between Milwaukee and Madison, Wisconsin, has become our Ice Age National Park. In the North Cascades of the State of Washington rounded ridges were shaped by glaciers and stand today in sharp contrast to the rough peaks farther south and west. The Ice Age left everything untouched south of Philadelphia, and that is why much of Appalachia, including the Smokies in Tennessee and the Blue Ridge in North Carolina, are so rich in plant life, for while glaciers kept the north frozen, the Atlantic south flourished and continued the endless process of subspeciation, which continues to this day and over the millennia has given our southern domain the greatest variety of flora on this continent.

The word *day* in Genesis is doubtless a figure of speech indicating a passage of time. And that *day*, so far as our plains and grass country are concerned, was eons. It took millennia to turn molten rock into soil. Wind erosion made deposits of fine particles that are measurable only in terms of centuries. Such are our loess deposits.

Water erosion and shifting stream channels created flood plains, on which seeds, traveling on planetary winds or carried by animals, were dropped, producing plants, grass, shrubs and trees. These flora—living, dying, and decaying—added to the humus, and so the soils were built, aided of course by earthworms and fertilized by the droppings and by the flesh and bones of beasts of the valleys. The chernozem, or black soil, was built by hundreds of plants, by fungi, insects and bacteria; by mammals and birds all working in harmony for tens of thousands of years.

Americans inherited rich topsoil—the black soil of the Middle West, foreordained to be the breadbasket of people on other continents, as well as those here. We grew grasses that were six feet high, making literally true the statement that grass grew higher than a man's stirrups. Civilization largely drove the tall grass out, and other species of grazing grass took its place. Today there still are some sections of the original prairie, and once plots are set aside as preserves, as some are in western Illinois, this tall grass returns. Yet in our ignorance we leveled the prairie, depriving it of its fertility, which over the centuries turns not on a single crop but on a multicrop habitat that has in it hundreds of members of an interlocked community that alone can perpetuate the prairie.

Much of our farmland was heavily wooded; clearing it was the settlers' first task. Areas such as Ohio were thick with hardwood forests, unique in variety and beauty. Yet so great was the hunger for land that few acres of the great hardwoods were preserved as reminders of the original America.

This original land teemed with wildlife, but man's intrusion was so pervasive and so persistent that some species have been wholly eliminated (notably the passenger pigeon), and some sixty are in danger of extinction. Buffalo were extinguished by mad slaughtering last century. Ducks and geese were close to extinction before mid-century and were saved by migratory bird legislation and watchful law enforcement. Vandalism in the ecological sense reached even into federal agencies. The Department of Agriculture gave bounties to those who would drain swamps or ponds, plant them with wheat, say for three years, and then remove them from production—receiving so much a year for *not growing wheat*. Thus even nesting areas of ducks and geese were depleted.

Free enterprise has long been the slogan of this nation and many preferences have been given it. Communities maneuvered to attract industry, and many choice farming areas were turned into factory sites, depriving the nation of a food-growing potential. Little or no thought was given to locating factories on sites that were not better suited to other uses, such as farming or recreation. Little thought or planning was given to the highest and best use, in the social sense, of each acre. The result was a hodge-podge, with metropolitan areas swallowed up by "development" and hardly any breathing space left. Choice valleys in New England, Ohio, California, Oregon and Washington were invaded by factories that might better have been placed on nearby waste lands. By 1970 the countryside of Americans was seriously imperiled. Vermont led the way with a statewide land-use program. The quality of life—not profit making only—emerged as a desirable standard for planning.

Pesticides have taken a deadly toll of our land. Many birds have been lost and some,

the peregrine falcon for example, are near extinction because of DDT and dieldrin.
These poisons have had an adverse effect on bacteria and fungi essential to soil building
and even on maggots, one of our foremost scavengers. Pesticides have caused drastic
declines in the bobwhite population, because they have killed insects highly charged
with the protein that the bobwhite needs. Sprays used to kill marijuana imperil the
pheasant population, for hemp seed is needed by the pheasants and other birds. Moreover, killing the marijuana plant deprives some areas of the nesting cover and protection
pheasants need.

Our Forest Service sprays mountain basins to get rid of sagebrush, but the herbicide
that kills it also kills willow on which moose and beaver depend. So a drastic change
in the life structure of alpine basins is made in order, it is said, to cause grass improvement. Restricted grazing would serve the same purpose and keep the ecology intact.

Mercury, used to treat seeds, is a new terror, for it kills the birds that eat the seeds.
A deadly poison has been used to kill coyotes for the benefit of sheepmen, but the results are disastrous: every creature that feeds on the carcass also dies. The result in some
of our western forests is the disappearance of practically all big birds and small game,
save for the pine marten. We have eight million sheep on public lands. The grazing
rights are for nominal fees. The public lands are fenced and reseeded for the benefit of
the sheepmen, and the predators are slaughtered in wholesale quantities for the benefit
of sheepmen. The whole public domain is filled with poisons.

The impact of so-called civilization on wildlife has even deeper roots than man's
predatory tactics. Wildlife flourishes in a varied habitat of shrubs, forbs and grasses.
Now we farm the land clean, no longer tolerating the sunflower, thistle and pigeon
grass. By clean farming we create an ideal environment for a particular insect that
specializes in a particular crop. As a result of the creation of a single-purpose environment, South Dakota's pheasant population has dropped from 13 million in 1940 to
2 million at present.

The Great Plains of America and many of the mountainous slopes face new dangers.
The high price of oil and the shortage of domestic oil has increased the demand for coal.
Vast deposits of coal are found in thirteen states west of the Mississippi; some is relatively free of sulphur and therefore less menacing as an air pollutant when burned, but
much of it will vastly pollute the air. This coal lies in strata fairly close to the surface,
and that makes strip mining feasible.

American experience with strip mining in Appalachia has been tragic. Whole valleys
have been ruined, and the sulphuric acid produced has poisoned the land and killed
all life in the streams. Sulphuric acid is not the threat west of the Mississippi; there the
threat is salt. Some experts predict that great rivers like the Missouri will be as full of
brine as the Colorado is today. Strip mining also promises to turn the wondrous grasslands of the Great Plains into rubble. Temporary housing will be erected and thousands
of people will move in. Wildlife experts expect that in antelope country (Wyoming)
they will be greatly endangered. In other areas the great sandhill cranes will be in jeop-

ardy. All wildlife will of course be driven from the site of the coal operation and severely depleted. The working crews will be tempted to become poachers, and the building of roads into the site will increase the pressure for legal hunting.

Among the wildlife endangered are prairie dogs and black-footed ferrets. In prairie states such as North Dakota, deer, fox, coyotes, grouse, pheasant, rabbits and songbirds survive because of densely wooded ravines. Strip mining will destroy them by destroying their habitat. The problem of rehabilitating strip-mined areas is the great battleground. Rehabilitation involves more than restoring the environment where grasslands will reappear and where grain can be grown. Wildlife habitats must, if possible, be reestablished. The experts seem to agree that technically mined areas can be rehabilitated where the rainfall is greater than ten inches. Even that involves staggering problems. Tens of thousands of years have produced only a few inches of topsoil. Unless that thin layer is somehow preserved in the mining and restored to the surface, the new surface will be raw, unweathered soil that is highly sodic. Once that sodic soil is leveled and shaped to meet the standards of rehabilitation, it solidifies in a crust after rain and becomes almost as impervious to water as concrete. Rehabilitation will take decades, perhaps centuries. It can be done, but it takes money and patience.

There are other likely awful effects of strip mining in the western states. The coal that is mined is commonly crushed into dust, slurried, and transported by pipeline to gasification plants, some hundreds of miles away. One gasification plant in North Dakota alone will produce 250 million cubic feet of gas daily. Ten million tons of coal a year will be consumed by it. Gasification plants promise to be a scourge when it comes to air pollution. Moreover, they consume large quantities of water in the conversion process. Water, in an area already short of water, becomes critical. Where will these semidesertic sites get the water? Deep wells, some five thousand feet deep, have been dug; rivers already needed for irrigation and municipal supplies are being tapped; the eyes of the promoters are now on the huge reservoirs built on tributaries of the main rivers.

We promise to pay an awful price merely to keep on our great energy "binge." The prospect of rubble where green grass and endless pasture land now meet the eye is appalling.

The Great Plains, including the heart of the Great American Desert, already has vast open-pit mining of copper. The new scars on the terrain are so enormous they can be seen for miles, and the dust from the hauling and the fumes from the plants are greatly polluting the air of Arizona, Nevada and Utah—air that once was our proudest boast. It sometimes seems that except where the people are vigilant and rise up in wrath, the big corporations are more powerful than government itself.

The mining threat encompasses not only coal and copper but vast mountain slopes in Colorado and Wyoming that have what is known as "shale oil." These shale deposits will be dug out with gargantuan shovels and put through rock crushers and presses to get the oil for which America has a great thirst. The prospect of putting much of two of the most beautiful of the fifty states through a rock crusher is appalling.

The environmental problem confronting humans has subtle connections with man's choice of violence to solve international problems and domestic problems as well. Axes and plows are for amateurs. We have been able to speed up the destructive cycle with bulldozers, high explosives, deep drilling, air compressors and the like. We can now do in a decade the damage it took the ancients centuries to accomplish.

Our violence can be horrendous, as when we use nuclear devices to dredge for us, or create huge craters that are radioactive for a thousand years by underground testing of our nuclear warheads. Our violence is quiet and unobtrusive, yet nonetheless lethal, when we pour industrial wastes into our waters or bury nuclear wastes in the ground.

The driving force behind the National Park Service is the concessionaires, who have annual permits to run hotels, provide parking space, sell food and drinks, run pack-trains for visitors, and the like. They have a financial stake in "mass movements" into the parks and encourage all devices that promote that end. They are indeed the favored few, for they are the only ones who can receive under park service rules notice and hearings of changes in accustomed ways of doing business. They are favored because "mass recreation" is favored. The park service loves its "mass recreation" statistics, and promotions are made on that basis. The hikers, campers and environmental groups are bothersome outsiders who have no right to notice and hearing. The drive for urbanization of the wilderness is a curse of national park management.

The national forests are largely considered to be croplands. Virgin timber, sorely needed for wilderness areas and for watershed protection, is being cut almost daily with Forest Service permission.

Buffer areas around true wilderness areas (roadless areas) are being sheared by the Forest Service, which means that roads will now reach the edges of the "wilderness," which means in turn that jeeps and motorcycles ("tote goats") will roar into the sanctuary and tear it up.

The Forest Service is now cutting timber up to ten thousand feet, where it takes 400 years and more to grow a tree. Even at two thousand feet it often takes 180 years to grow a merchantable ponderosa pine in certain areas of the Pacific West.

A 1970 report of the Montana School of Forestry points out that in the Bitterroots the Forest Service cutting is on steep and rugged terrain where it is uneconomical to grow new stands. The Forest Service, it says, is engaged in "timber mining."

Clear-cutting the forests (in which every tree is cut in areas as large as a section of land) is the practice in most areas; and, where pine is involved, the clear-cutting is followed by burning the slash to promote regeneration; but that exposes the mineral soil and results in great erosion. Where clear-cutting is in Douglas fir and hemlock, the new undergrowth includes many berries that bears find attractive. Yet bears also occasionally strip the bark off a young sapling for its sweet cambium layer. Hence lumber companies hired hunters, who killed most of the bears. The Montana report said that "consideration of recreation, watershed, wildlife and grazing appear as afterthoughts" to Forest Service management.

The service, entrusted with protecting the public interest in national forest lands, has become lumber-minded and has lost sight of "the entire spectrum of forest-related values," to use the words of Senator Gale W. McGee of Wyoming. Big and small lumber companies hold great sway over the Forest Service. The training of foresters orients them to lumber and logging. The pressure group they see every day is the timbermen. Their local (district) offices are close to the community and sensitive to the desire of even the gyppo, or small speculative logger, who, if he can cut Sunrise Creek, will put eight men to work. Lumber companies often reward "cooperative" Forest Service personnel with lucrative executive positions on retirement or even sooner. The Forest Service is so wedded to the lumber industry that public protests, to be successful, must produce a veritable gale that blows through the inbred, commercial-minded Forest Service.

The lumber industry now speaks of its "rightful" interest in national forest trees. But they have no "right" to that subsidy, any more than sheepmen and cattlemen have the "right" to graze on the lands, or miners, the "right" to minerals on public lands. The "right" is that of "we the people" who own these forests.

The Forest Service for years has been under a mandate to guard the national forests for multiple use: "for outdoor recreation, range, timber, watershed, and wildlife and fish purposes." The Forest Service in a 1971 report conceded that the uses other than timber production have not been protected. The reasons given are interesting: the lack of trained men, the lack of adequate budget, the lack of understanding of the needs of wildlife, the protection of soils, the improvement of air and water quality, and the promotion of all other multiple uses. Reading this Forest Service apologia will make even a Forest Service fan come full circle and realize that the public trust is being abused.

The forests are very seldom flat bottomlands. In the Far West, they are on steep mountainsides that are ecologically fragile even when covered with stable forests.

There is no timber shortage. Several billion board feet of our timber are exported yearly, and housing goals can be met without any increase in timber production. The truth is that lumber consumption is declining. It has indeed been static since 1910 despite our mounting population. To enable the lumber industry to hang onto the market, we place our forest lands on the sacrificial block. We now think of forestry as being either profitable and therefore desirable, or unprofitable and therefore undesirable.

Multiple use has become a misnomer. Land used for a highway preempts all other use. Land used for strip mining is the same. Certain types of logging or even grazing may ruin most, if not all, other uses. The idea of multiple use is to honor all uses when the land is put to a particular use. Watershed values, stream protection, the safeguarding of wildlife, recreational uses by man—these should not be materially impaired by any other dominant use. Yet logging in the Far West has increased the sedimentation of streams, at times wiping out salmon runs. That is not multiple use. Open-pit mining not only destroys esthetic qualities but pollutes the streams and causes untold erosion by runoffs of water. That is not multiple use. Multiple use has been so perverted by the federal regime that a new standard is needed.

The dollar policy that seeks to convert every possible tree into money has all but ruined our national forests. What we need is an ecological standard: stabilization of water supplies, production of atmospheric oxygen, protection of flora, fauna and topsoils, preservation of outdoor recreation, and salvaging the spiritual values inherent in scenic beauty and the wonders of the woods.

America needs ecological forestry management, not dollar forestry that lines a few pockets with money. Entomologists warn that a pure stand (a single species forest) forms an ideal situation for damage from insects and disease; infection is rapid and direct from tree to tree, and if one species is destroyed, there is nothing left. A mono-culturally managed forest creates the need for pesticides and herbicides and the biotic diversity is destroyed. The Council on Environmental Quality once proposed that clear-cutting be drastically regulated but the timber lobby defeated it.

Americans complained about reckless logging practices during the administration of President Theodore Roosevelt, prior to the advent of the Forest Service. Yet what was done in our early years was minuscule compared with what goes on today. Last century lumber companies were cutting thirteen hundred acres of redwoods a year. In the 1960s they were cutting thirteen thousand acres of redwoods a years, which averages out at one thousand redwood trees a day. Once Congress passed the Redwood National Park Act in 1968, the redwood industry began to cut feverishly—twelve hours a day, six days a week with the most destructive techniques known to man. The cutting went to the edge of the park, so that there would be no incentive to expand the park.

Sentiment grows (1) to put an end to large-block clear-cutting, (2) to use selective cutting, (3) never to small patch cut for over 40 acres, (4) to ban logging above the three-thousand-foot level, (5) to put down for public hearings any proposal to cut public lands so that ecological considerations may be weighed against the dollar profit, (6) to ban the use of all herbicides, and (7) to recycle all paper and paper products. It is estimated that if we recycle only 50 percent of these paper wastes, we can save 90 million acres of timberland for recreational, wildlife and watershed use.

Land can also be recycled. Cut-over lands, if set aside as wilderness, would in time be returned by nature to their original beauty, where temperature, water and sun provide the necessary environment. Temperature, sun and water can rejuvenate waste lands and provide the basic healing that is needed, provided man stands back and lets nature take over.

The possibilities of reclaiming waste lands or renovating them for new uses are infinite. The need to do so will increase as the population mounts and even remote trails become so crowded with hikers that at long last every campsite in the high country is regulated under a permit system. Indeed the Forest Service in 1971 required permits for one to enter overcrowded wilderness areas in California, and in 1972 the park service started regulating the number of people who could visit the back-country areas.

The trails of some wilderness areas should be open to travel either by horseback or by backpacking. Horses, however, present special problems. They may trample a small meadow to death. Some areas have insufficient horse feed, making it necessary to pack horse feed in. We must soon classify wilderness areas for the type of use permitted.

That is one zoning problem; there are others. Most wilderness areas need to be protected from sheep and cattle. That is true of the Cascades in Washington and Oregon and the Wallowas in eastern Oregon, all of which still bear the awful scars of unrelenting grazing that reached its peak about 1910.

Tote goats should be banned from most trails, as they raise havoc with people, horses and wildlife and chew the trails to dust. When allowed into high basins they churn them into desert bowls in only a few hours. Racing like mad, they destroy the delicate, exquisite beauties of the high country in only a few hours. If allowed, they must be restricted to lowland trails and roads where the damage is already done.

The complete abolition of snowmobiles from wilderness areas or roads leading into them is mandatory. They are impossible to patrol and do untold damage.

A few lakes, but only a few, might allow floatplanes. But generally they should be banned from all waters in wilderness areas, and the same ban should be put on helicopters operating in the high country. The early experience with the Quetico-Superior region in northern Minnesota proved conclusively that if private or commercial planes and helicopters are not banned, the solitude of the wilderness will be destroyed, and potbellied urbanites will fly into lakes in such numbers as to destroy quiet, solitude and fishing for everyone else.

Mining must be banned from wilderness areas. Mining means roads and roads mean the invasion of vehicles that marks the end of wilderness.

Some people in government, and some out, want our mountain retreats developed in the manner of Switzerland. That would destroy the sanctuaries for which this continent has been famous.

All roads must be kept out of the high country. It must be reserved as the special reward to our great-great grandchildren, who will see it as Daniel Boone, Henry Thoreau and John Muir once saw it. They should be able to discover and appreciate the America that once was but that the machine has largely destroyed.

Some say that the maintenance of wilderness areas favors the rich and discriminates against the poor, that only by opening up the sanctuaries with roads can the poor receive the benefits of the wilderness that the rich enjoy. But this rich-poor syndrome is a myth. The costs associated with wilderness recreation (apart from skiing) are comparable to or lower than those associated with other outdoor recreation. The cost of wilderness travel on foot is certainly no more than five dollars a day. The choice of wilderness recreation turns not on income but on taste preferences. Money does not form tastes, nor does wilderness price even the poor out of the market.

National parks and national forests should have roads only on their perimeters, leaving the inner sanctuaries untouched. All civilization can be contained there. The motels, hotels and campgrounds on the perimeter can be the take-off points for those sturdy enough and brave enough to venture into the interior.

No zoning should be done by administrative fiat. The people own the public lands, and if they choose to turn each park or forest into a New York City Central Park, that is their prerogative. If they so decide, the future will indeed be gruesome. But I have a deep faith that our people will not want to destroy the great American outdoors, an important segment of our spiritual heritage and the greatest bit of outdoors in the world.

Since World War II there has been an increasing interest in the American wilderness by people in general. Recreational appetites have increased, and more and more people turn their faces to the woods and to the mountains. This trend is partly due to the increased number of roads that pierce the vastness of our mountains, some built for logging or mining, some for general highway use. The increase of highways has been so great that only in a few areas (Alaska excepted) can one get more than ten miles from a road.

Visitations to the mountains in most areas are for picnic purposes or for camping in areas where the campground leaves space for the automobile or motorcycle and where it supplies an outdoor table, a fireplace, pure water and toilet facilities. A single one of these campgrounds, especially in national parks, may attract on a summer day twenty thousand or more people.

This is a campground community, ever changing but leaving no space for a family who arrives at dusk. While these campgrounds are usually in national parks; national forests commonly have less pretentious ones. They too are jampacked by people with autos, especially on summer weekends. State parks and state forests are numerous, but they are not as large as their federal counterparts. Measured by the number of people and cars seeking campgrounds in the mountainous areas, we are in very short supply.

The auto camper is not the true measure of the demand. Back-country use, either by mule or horse trains or by backpacking, is probably twenty times what it was in the late forties. Remote trails, quite distant from any road, are fairly saturated with backpackers. Some of our high alpine country even in the nine- to eleven-thousand-foot zone has already been so heavily tramped by people on foot as to imperil the ecological health of those areas. Supplies of wood for campfires is scarce at higher elevations. Sanitation facilities are often lacking. The topsoil is skimpy and fragile. It will take decades to make a burn from even one campfire disappear.

Another problem is raised by winter use of mountainous areas. Snowmobiles are now common. A snowmobile will double or treble the domain of a trapper looking for beaver, but snowmobile damage to other game is considerable. When the deep snow comes, deer and elk are in a precarious condition. Life itself is at a low ebb. They have runways in the snow leading to browse, such as willow and Douglas maple. Snowmobilers chase the wildlife in their runways to the point of exhaustion. This is wanton slaughter of animals that have only a narrow margin for survival in the wintertime. In the lower areas snowmobiles have raced across meadows that are private property in which the owners have established tree farms. Snowmobiles rushing across these areas snip off the tips of the young trees, which may be only barely visible on the snow's surface. A snowmobiler often spends hours circling a house. His pleasure is at the expense of the householder, who came to the winter woods for peace and quiet and is tempted to use the shotgun.

Winter use by skiers has greatly multiplied in recent decades. Mountain areas with sparse snow are equipped with machines that make snow for the skiers. Those endowed with an early snowfall begin the skiing season in November and it may last until April. A spectacular increase in ski lifts and lodges has brought millions to ever-increasing sites for this winter recreation. This winter invasion of the wilderness has also taken a toll. The building of ski runs means cutting broad swathes down steep hillsides and thus increasing the problems of erosion. The building of lodges down one range (as for example the Green Mountains of Vermont) has increased the sewage pollution problems of rural areas. These problems are manageable and the commitment of Americans to this form of recreation is a deep and permanent one.

Summer and winter recreational use has increased at an exponential rate. It has brought home to most people that the recreational demands exceed the recreational facilities. Hence proposals are recurring (1) to protect more and more areas from the saws of the lumber interests, (2) to provide larger areas for the diverse recreational needs of the people, and (3) to control more strictly the summer and winter use of the woods and the mountainous areas by motorized vehicles.

Alaska presents new and serious problems. It remains our last unspoiled wilderness. It is vast, stretching across four time zones; it is 90 percent uninhabited by man. The total space occupied by lakes in Alaska is 11 thousand square miles. Alaska has Mount McKinley, our highest mountain, and a dozen or more other great peaks and probably more volcanoes than any other area in the world. Alaska has vast uncharted forests and countless rivers that are largely unexplored. It has the greatest abundance of fish and wildlife in the entire continent. Dahl sheep occupy the Brooks Range. Grizzly and brown bears, wolves, wolverines and fox roam the wilds of Alaska. It is the nesting ground for many birds, some of which come way up from Antarctica to raise their young and then fly back south. Alaska has the biggest known glaciers on earth, so large it is estimated that one fifth of the earth's fresh water is locked up in them.

Those who are out to get rich have their eyes either on Alaska's lush timber, or on her oil and other deposits, or on her fishing potential. Thus Alaska for Americans is their last frontier. Will it be cruelly exploited by merchants and adventurers as were "the lower forty-eight" states? Or will it be managed according to an ecological ethic?

Those are unresolved questions as we enter 1975. But there is a mounting concern among our people that maximizing profits is not the way. Eternal America requires that the quality of life become the new standard. Then *America* will indeed become *Eternal*.

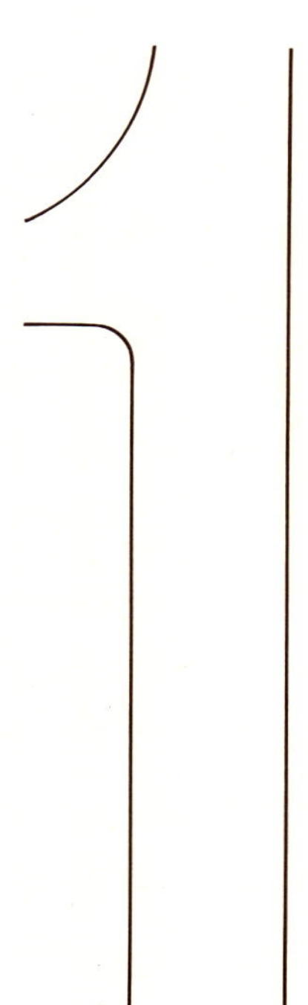

DAWN

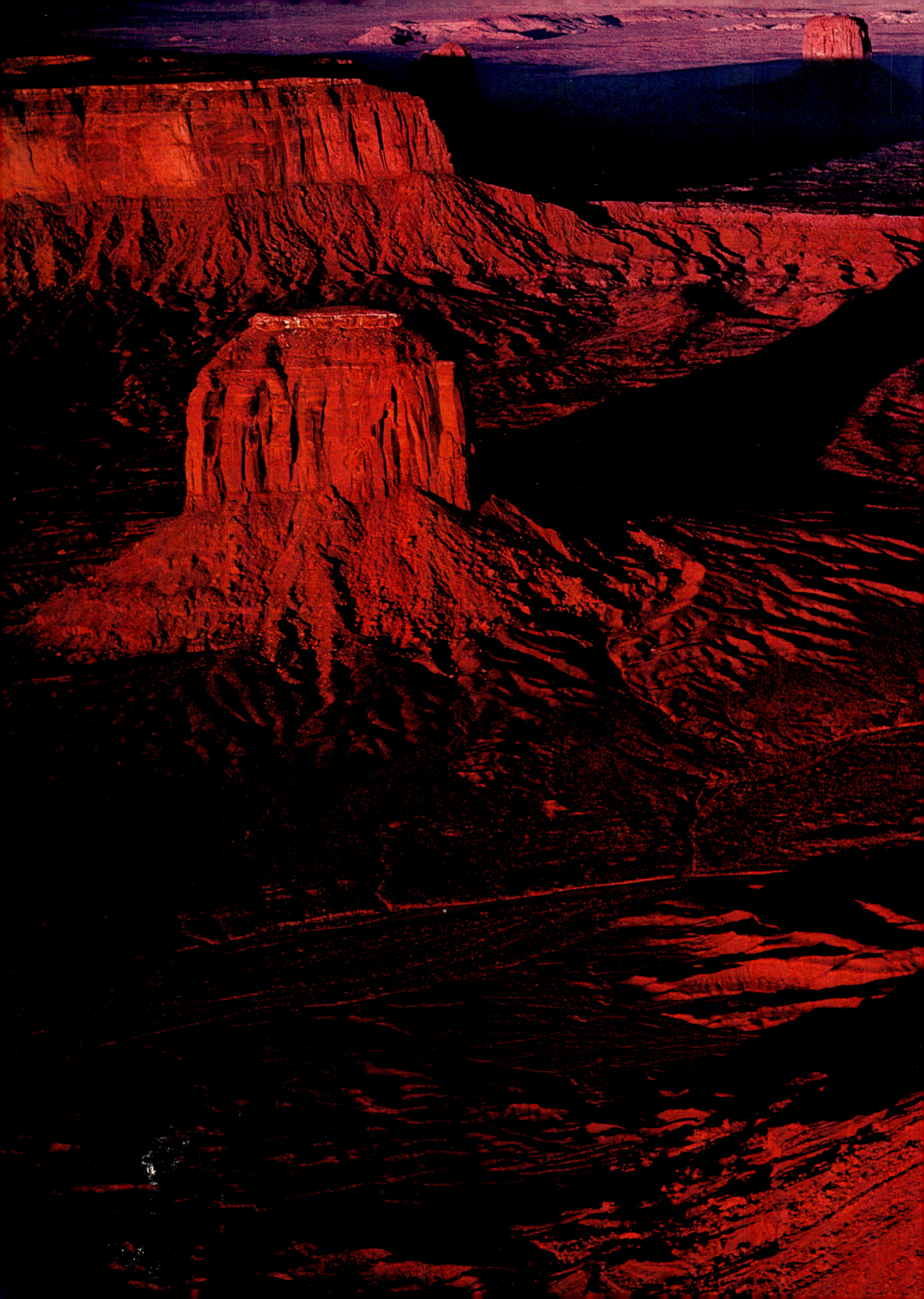

REMEMBERED SCENES OF MONUMENT VALLEY made an indelible impression on my mind. It was not at first a direct impression, for I had only seen the vast desert and towering buttes in a movie, John Ford's *Stagecoach*. Nevertheless, my mind was made up; someday I would see Monument Valley with my own eyes.

In 1958, I became the chief cameraman for Fuji Telecasting Company, but in the following year I took a leave of absence to become a special correspondent for the *Chūnichi Shimbun*. In this capacity, I was to make a trip around the world. My resolve to see that valley had not lessened, but there were obstacles to be overcome. In those days, foreign currency reserves were at an ebb, yen had to be converted into dollars—then the standard international currency—and the amount of money that those who were fortunate enough to be able to go abroad could take with them was limited.

Eventually the opportunity presented itself, and I managed to reach the town of Monticello, Utah, less than one hundred miles from Monument Valley. Since no bus service was available, I hitched a ride on a mail truck. This got me as far as Mexican Hat, near the border between Utah and Arizona. And there I was. I could find no transportation to take me the rest of the way.

Being only twenty-four years old, healthy and full of energy, I decided to set out on foot. While a photographer may at times travel alone, he does not go empty-handed. There being no other way, I shouldered my equipment and began the trip through the desert. The sun beat down; the heat was beyond belief. I had not gone a great distance before I found that I was completely exhausted. There in the distance, spires and buttes, red and rocky, soared into the sky, so near yet so far. Despite my youth, I could not go on.

With great reluctance, I picked myself up and retraced my steps from Mexican Hat. Many pictures have been drawn of the vastness of the American continent, even that portion of it encompassed by the borders of the United States, but that was the first time for me to experience the vastness that writers of words and drawers of pictures have attempted to describe. Both land and sky were enormous.

Several years passed before I was successful in entering Monument Valley. I was then at work on the photography of the United States for the twenty-six-volume *Sekai Bunka Shirizu* ("World Culture Series"). Hiring a jeep and a guide at Goulding's Lodge, Utah, I went to the valley and took pictures until my heart was content, at least for the time being.

In 1973, I was able to return to the valley three times, in the middle of March, late in July and in the middle of October, visiting Coin Valley and Hunt's Mesa for the first time and taking photographs not only from the ground but from the air. From the top of a uranium mine located out in the desert thirty-seven miles from Mexican Hat, I took pictures of Coin Valley. When I returned in the summer and fall, I again photographed Monument Valley; Hunt's Mesa makes an excellect viewing platform. The view of mesas and buttes stretched out laterally in a long row is spectacular, but getting there presents difficulties. Roads, frequently washed out in rainstorms, are left unrepaired and abandoned. We were the only ones there.

We (my three assistants and myself) were fortunate to be able to enlist the services of Navajo rangers, who provided us with a jeep and acted as guides. The rock formations in the valley are only fifteen to sixteen hundred feet in height, but the inclines in some places are nearly 45 degrees. Although our vehicle was powerful enough to make the climb, it was difficult for me to understand how rangers were able to find their way to the top of the mesas. It must have been due to their traditions as a people and their long familiarity with the land.

During the summer, my trips to Hunt's Mesa lasted only one day; in the fall, I camped atop the mesa in a tent. The splendor of the valley was not the only view. There was also the starry vault of heaven. I had, for long periods of time, camped in the Alps and the Himalayas. In fact, I had spent nearly four years camping alone in the Himalayas at altitudes of from six to nine thousand feet. But not once had I seen the night sky so beautiful; never had the stars shone so brilliantly.

The silence, too, was different. It was absolute. In the Himalayas, the wind strikes the steep walls and knifelike ridges and howls incessantly. And when it dies down, the stillness is metallic, brooding, frozen. Here in the desert, the silence spoke tranquillity, even warmth. Had it not been for the tasks that still lay before me, I would have provided myself with food and water and stayed on for weeks.

For my photographs of Monument Valley (approximately twelve hundred in number), I used a supertelephoto lens and concentrated on the sun as it rose and the sun as it set, in combination with the rocks of the earth.

With a 4800-mm lens, an error of even a few inches in setting up the two tripods means disaster. One of the most difficult problems is determining the position of the sun, which varies not only from season to season but from day to day. Real photography could begin only on the second day of each visit; even then I made mistakes. And if the weather was bad for two or three days, I had to start all over again.

While I could select a position before dawn, the light on the horizon was difficult to read, for the sun did not seem to rise vertically. Rather it seemed to lean to the south. After catching sight of the glow, I had to drive as much as a fifth of a mile to a new position, and then I had only a few seconds to take the picture I wanted. Practice made the difference.

I used a 6-by-7-cm camera for a number of reasons, and one of them was the size of the sun. With a 1000-mm lens, the diameter of the sun on the film is about 1 centimeter; with a 4800-mm lens, this increases to 4.8 centimeters. If a 35-mm camera is used, the frame is not large enough for anything but the sun.

Other areas where I found the mesas photogenic were Arches National Park and Lake Powell in the Glen Canyon National Recreation Area, each of which I visited three times. In the former, the rock was formed some 150 million years ago, during the Jurassic period, when life was just emerging from the sea and just before dinosaurs began to roam the continent. Sand solidified into rock under enormous pressure was eroded into windows and arches by wind and water. The patterns, singularly and in the aggregate, are fantastic, and I was thunderstruck by the extraordinary moods they give rise to. Leaving my motel in Moab before the crack of dawn every day, I took photographs of arches and the rising sun, later breakfasted in the solitude of the picnic area. How delicious the food tasted, how good the air!

At Lake Powell, too, which I photographed from the air, the scenes were fantastic, transcending reality. No trees, not a blade of grass as far as the eye could see, the rocky spires red in the morning glow above the surface of the lake: I doubted that I was on the planet I thought I was on. Particularly in the fall was I able to fix this image perfectly on film.

My jumping-off place had been Los Angeles, which I had left in a driving rain on February 4, 1973. During the eighteen months prior to that, I had been convalescent and had had time to think over my lifework, the theme of which has been the regeneration of the human spirit through the rediscovery of the earth. The American continent, I thought, fitted this image, so

I read everything I could on the natural sights of the United States. Eventually, I selected thirty-seven places, centered primarily on national parks and national monuments.

Death Valley was my first stop. It seemed to be a small park in a valley, but I was soon astonished by its vastness. Although it is only 125 miles long from north to south, during the eight days we were there, we drove 1,000 miles. From Dante's View, 5,475 feet above sea level, and Badwater, 282 feet below sea level, and Devil's Golf Course, the views were fine. However, the place that challenged my camera was the Mesquite Flat sand dunes at Stove Pipe Wells.

Despite the fact that we went there three times (in the winter, fall and spring), no matter how many pictures I took, none of them was really satisfactory. I had seen pictures taken by Edward Weston, Ansel Adams and others—masterpieces of the sand dunes—and I had a fervent desire to do as well. Yet the dunes at Stove Pipe Wells were elusive, uncaptureable. I began my photography by having a good look around under the guidance of rangers, chartering a plane and walking in the dunes. I came back in April, on my way from Zion National Park to Los Angeles.

The dark gray sand itself is nothing, at least for color photography, until, a quarter hour after sunrise and just before sunset, it is magically dyed pink and yellow. However, the dunes changing their features with the shifting of the sun's rays become excellent subjects for black and white photography. I had observed a similar phenomenon in the Alps and the Himalayas.

Between Zion National Park and Death Valley, we had seen tiny flowers of pink, yellow and white, growing profusely in the Arizona desert. I was preoccupied with Mesquite Flat and did not take any pictures. I regret that now, for I was told that the desert blooms only a few times in a hundred years.

Leaving Death Valley, we traveled through Las Vegas, stayed overnight in Kingman, Arizona, and arrived the next day at Saguaro National Monument, whose two sections lie east and west of Tucson. The reason that we spent two days to travel only five hundred miles was that we were not used to the superhighways. (The car and its pollution, the superhighway and its accidents have become popular more recently in Japan than they did in the United States.) We later covered as much as six hundred miles a day, so it can be seen how slow was our progress those two days.

Far more beautiful than the Rincon Mountain section of the national monument is the Tucson Mountain section to the west of the city. There are a number of small hills, and the saguaros stretch on and on, to the edges of the Sonora Desert. This cactus is the giant of the family, growing to heights of 40 and 50 feet and weighing as much as ten tons when mature, though its roots are shallow. Growth is not rapid. After the first ten years, the height is only about one inch; after reaching a height of 7 to 10 feet, the rate of growth is about four inches per year. After 50 to 75 years, blossoms come for the first time. Death comes at the age of 150 to 200 years, most often with uprooting by wind or flashfloods.

On my last day there, I photographed the saguaros in the sunrise. At ten o'clock, we finished breakfast, folded our tents, and decamped. Only six hours later we were four hundred miles away, in White Sands National Monument, where that evening I again focused my camera on sand dunes.

I had been there before, about sixteen years previously. On that occasion I had had only one hour for photography, and while I was running through the park, I was chased by rangers in a jeep. After hearing my explanation, their attitude changed and they became very kind.

Those photographs were carried in the magazine *Camera Art* and were the first to introduce White Sands as a place to Japan. It had been introduced in another way long before.

White Sands Missile Range, with all its secrets, surrounds the national monument. Before leaving Tokyo, I had obtained permission to take pictures from the air; I was the first civilian to do so (photography from the ground is permitted). However, there were conditions: an army officer was always nearby, the course of our plane was decided by the base, we were always tracked by radar, and my film had to be processed at the base's laboratory. I am happy to say that all my pictures were "safe" and were returned to me.

East of the park is an air base, from which Phantom fighters rose and returned to earth. I was surprised that I could aim my camera in that direction, but, at times, was not permitted to photograph the desolation of the desert to the west. The prohibited times seemed to depend on the altitude of our plane. It seemed to me that the desert does indeed hold many secrets.

The sand is gypsum and pure white, washed down from the San Andres Mountains into Lake Lucero and then picked up by the wind when the water evaporates. A third of the estimated 15 billion tons has been shipped off as construction material and is now in the fireproof walls of skyscrapers in New York and a hundred other cities. Not far away, as distances go in America, the atomic bomb that later fell on Hiroshima was first tested.

Later I visited southern Utah. In contrast to the white gypsum, the fine particles in the Coral Pink Sand Dunes were blazingly bright, so much so that my eyes hurt. It is difficult to express in words my wonder at what the gods have created out of nature.

color plates

Monument Valley in the Morning Glow
This valley on the Utah-Arizona border spreads over 1,500 square miles in the much larger Navajo Indian Reservation but has only a few places that are photogenic. Although I visited the valley in winter and summer, not until October was I able to capture the rocky buttes in the variegated hues of the morning glow. Taking off in a Cessna before dawn, we circled lazily until, with the first rays of the sun, the desert sprang to life. On the right are the Mitten Buttes; to the left is Merrick Butte, all rising about 1,600 feet from the floor of the desert.

Turret Arch from North Window
Natural, eroded-stone arches and windows in Arches National Park, approximately ninety in number, lie in three sections known as Courthouse Tower, the Windows and Devil's Garden. From North Window, where this photograph was taken early on a midsummer morning, South Window is immediately to the left. It did not, as I had expected, turn out red. I took pictures of the crimson arch three times during the fall; on comparing them, I felt that this one, though more subdued, has much greater depth. This national park is near Moab, Utah.

Stagecoach and Castle Buttes
We flew over these buttes in Monument Valley scores of times in order to take this picture on a clear evening in the middle of October. In the Himalayas, composing a picture while on the ground was easier, because of the size of the mountains. Here it was impossible to compose a perfect picture if the course of the plane veered even slightly. As the shadows lengthened, we reduced altitude, but because of the speed of the plane, it was difficult to maintain a balance between rocks and shadows. This was the moment when they turned bright yellow.

Window Section in Hailstorm
In Arches National Park one evening in October, while the lightning flashed and the thunder rolled, unseasonal hailstones fell like a torrent from the black clouds above. Putting on my hat, gloves and a feather-lined jacket I used for mountain climbing, I took several pictures of the storm. Then, looking back, I saw the Window section glowing red. As the storm passed, the color died quickly from the left. In the center, the window with a tower is Turret Arch. North Window is to the left. This is the eastern half of the Window section.

Afterglow
The butte on the left is Stagecoach, the small one in the center is Rabbit and Bear Rock, and the one on the right is Castle Butte (Monument Valley). As the shadows lengthened, only the rocks and horizon glowed a deep red. This was my last shutter chance before, in a matter of seconds, the light was gone. After taking this picture, we turned back to see the whole valley sink into a gray world of death. I thought to myself that it must be a drama of light staged by nature, for the scene minutes before had belonged to a different realm.

Lake Powell
This aerial photograph was taken from the east just after sunrise. From its headwaters in the Rocky Mountains, the Colorado River flows southeast of Arches National Park, continues through the middle of Canyonlands National Park, and enters Glen Canyon National Recreation Area, where it forms Lake Powell. Mesas and buttes, bright yellow and red in the morning and evening glow, rise in majestic beauty above the surface of the lake. Of hundreds of photographs taken in the spring, summer and fall, I think the fall ones are the best.

Mesa in Monument Valley

Into this world of silence the only sound that comes is the evening wind whistling through the grass. The wind is called pinion and juniper. On the horizon at the left is Eagle Mesa; the slender rock to the left is Eagle Rock. Brigham's Tomb is in the center, and the two rocks rising from the triangular rock are King on a Throne. To the right of these are Stagecoach Butte and Rabbit and Bear Rock and then Castle Butte, which is also known as the Cathedral. On the extreme right is Big Bic Indian. This was taken from near Goulding's Lodge, Utah.

Window Section and the Moon

The three windows, from left to right, are North Window, South Window and, resembling the eye of a needle, Turret Arch. The only place from which the three can be viewed simultaneously is a parking lot a little beyond Courthouse Tower. After climbing the cliffs and walking about fifteen minutes to the edge of the plateau, I took pictures in the evening glow. As I was about to leave, the moon came up, so I reassembled my photographic equipment for this picture. The exposure was seven seconds. (Arches National Park.)

Bear Rock and the Sun

To take a picture of the sun at dawn is easy; to capture sun and rocks together is not. Every morning, the sun would come up in a different position, which varied by about two and one half times its diameter. Using a 6-by-7-cm camera with a 4800-mm telephoto lens (requiring two tripods), I would sit in the car with the engine running and, when the sun rose, drive at full speed to the proper position. Since I had only ten seconds, it was necessary to practice this many times. A good test shot one day did not, unfortunately, guarantee success the next day.

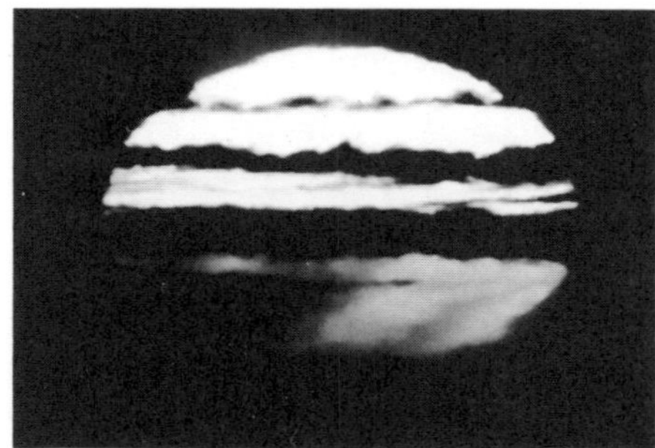

Sunrise in the Desert

Rain screened the lower part of the sun, turning it into liquid. It looked ready to melt and fall down. Nearer the stormy earth, rain fell to the rumble of thunder from one of the black-striped clouds dotting the eastern horizon. I had set out to photograph Ship Rock, when the sun rose over the San Juan Basin. This is southeast of Four Corners, where the borders of Arizona, Colorado, New Mexico and Utah meet (the only point in the country common to four states); the region is famous for its scenery. I used a 4800-mm telephoto lens.

Forest of Saguaro

Only after seventy-five years of growth does the saguaro bear branches. The mature cactus weighs from six to ten tons, of which one ton is water. This picture was taken in the evening from a hill near the Sus Picnic Area in the Tucson Mountain section of Saguaro National Monument. Between this western section (24 square miles) and the eastern Rincon Mountain section (98 square miles) lies the city of Tucson, Arizona. The growth of cactus in this western part, which lies east of the Sonora Desert, is older than that in the other part.

Death Valley I

Three thousand square miles of this desert in California and Nevada are included in Death Valley National Monument. Badwater, 282 feet below sea level, is the lowest surface depression in the Western Hemisphere. Annual precipitation is about two inches, and water that runs down from the mountains is quickly soaked up or evaporates. Although I took aerial photographs, I think the ones taken from the ground are the best. In this one, the rays of the evening sun bring into beautiful relief the patterns on the sand, freshened earlier by a strong wind.

Death Valley II

This picture was taken in late October, on the third and last of my visits to Death Valley. Every day we went into the dunes early in the morning and in the evening. As we walked along in Mesquite Flat, I was thinking that it was not a good place for photography. Then, as the sun was about to disappear below the Panamint Range, I changed my mind, thinking that if I did not take a picture, I would lose the chance. The footprints seen, unfortunately, in the upper part of the photograph, taken in a southwesterly direction, are mine and my two assistants'.

black & white plates

Delicate Arch

This is the symbol of Arches National Park in Utah. The rocks here were formed during the Jurassic period, more than 100 million years before the appearance of man on earth. Ever so slowly, wind and water eroded the stone into arches and windows, delicately formed and beautifully balanced. Here on a high mountain, they are freestanding. In order to make a vertical composition, I took this picture from the side, making the arch appear narrower than it actually is. The backlighting comes from sunlight streaming through the arch.

Double O Arch

Although there is a parking lot only three miles away, to arrive at this point in the spectacular, innermost reaches of the Devil's Garden in Arches National Park, one follows a hiking trail, walking along the edges of cliffs and climbing over huge boulders. A sign warns that anyone without hiking experience should not attempt it. As the name implies, there are two zeros, a very large one over a rather small one; the black, round shadow underneath outlines a circle when seen from the front. Despite its apparent artificiality, it is the work of nature.

Turret Arch and the Moon

When the sun rose, the moon was still high in the heavens. It continued to shine brilliantly in the blue sky even after the sun turned the arch red. As it approached the horizon, its edges became indistinct, as if it were melting. By the time it sank below the horizon just before noon, I had taken more than one hundred photographs, some with telephoto and wide-angle lenses. I recalled the moon seen through the smog-filled sky of Tokyo, where it looks like a bloody disc. Where nature holds sway, it is beautiful. This is the east side of Turret Arch.

Mitten Buttes and Merrick Butte

These buttes, Mitten to the left and center, Merrick to the right, are representative of the scenery in Monument Valley. With the thumb separated from the four fingers, the two buttes do indeed resemble hands in mittens. Not far from here, there is a campground, a park office has been constructed, and because traffic has become quite heavy, stakes have been driven along the roadside. Shadows of the stakes were troublesome when I took pictures in the evening. It is sad to think how difficult it has become to photograph the earth in its natural state.

Bear and Rabbit Rock

As recently as sixty million years ago, this area was covered by a sea that extended from the Gulf of Mexico to the Arctic Ocean. Viewed from the entrance to Monument Valley, these formations look like the animals after which they are named, but the resemblance is lost in this aerial photograph, taken in the early morning as we approached from the east. On the left is Rabbit rock and Bear rock is to the right. Although comparatively small, they are delicately formed. Mute evidence of the creativity of the forces of nature is the hole in Bear rock.

White Sands

The U.S. Army's missile range just west of Alamogordo, New Mexico, completely surrounds White Sands National Monument. The weight of the gypsum in the monument alone has been calculated to be 15 billion tons. Winds picking up sand left by the evaporating waters of Lake Lucero continually add to the dunes. Permission for aerial photography is difficult to obtain. An officer flew with us, and we were monitored on radar. For Japanese, the area is chillingly unforgettable, for here the atomic bomb dropped on Hiroshima was first tested.

Great Sand Dunes

While I was trying to focus my camera, it jumped up and hit me in the nose and forehead. Even trying to sit still in the plane was a great effort, due to the turbulence of the air currents over the desert. (Winds of great strength are, of course, the shapers of the dunes.) The shaking of the plane is sometimes violent enough to result in injury. This early morning photograph was taken in a northeasterly direction from the skies above Great Sand Dunes National Monument. Just to the east is the range of mountains known as Sangre de Cristo.

Death Valley III

Footprints on the sand running from left to right in the center of the picture are those of small birds, which I did not find objectionable. But human footprints were another matter. After the departure of tourist buses, I had to wait for one week for the irregularly wandering marks to disappear from the sand. This happened most often during my visit in the spring. (I also made visits in the summer and fall.) In the far distance, Corkscrew Peak (5,804 feet) is in the center. Unknown Peak (6,117) is to the left of that; Thimble Peak (6,381) is on the extreme left.

Death Valley IV

More than five hundred square miles of the valley lie below sea level. The scanty rainfall comes mostly in cloudbursts, and for days on end in the summer, temperatures between 120 and 130 degrees are common. Seekers after gold are among those who have perished here. Beyond the dunes in the upper part of the picture, the road connecting Stove Pipe Wells and Furnace Creek runs from left to right. Leaving our car on the road, we walked for about fifty minutes into the wilderness. This is an evening picture. Winters are relatively mild.

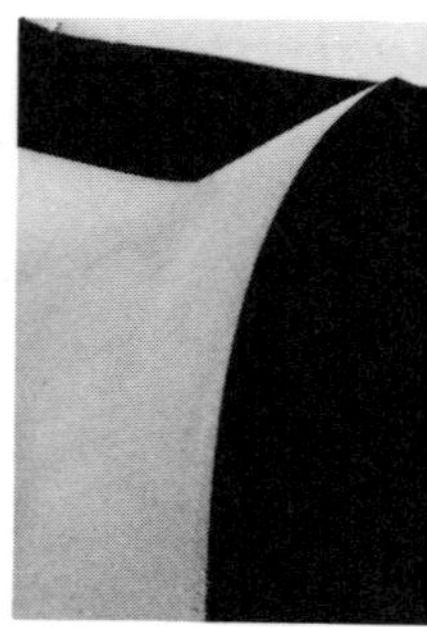

Death Valley V

Scores of shifting low ridges and shallow depressions are the prominent features of the sand dunes. Five or six years ago, the ridges ran eastwards and westwards; now they run in a north-south direction. It took only a day or so for a blinding windstorm to change their direction. From visits in the winter and spring, I remembered quite clearly the shape of the dunes. I was amazed to return in the fall and find their shapes completely altered. From the lowest point in the desert to Mount Whitney (14,494 feet), the distance is seventy-five miles.

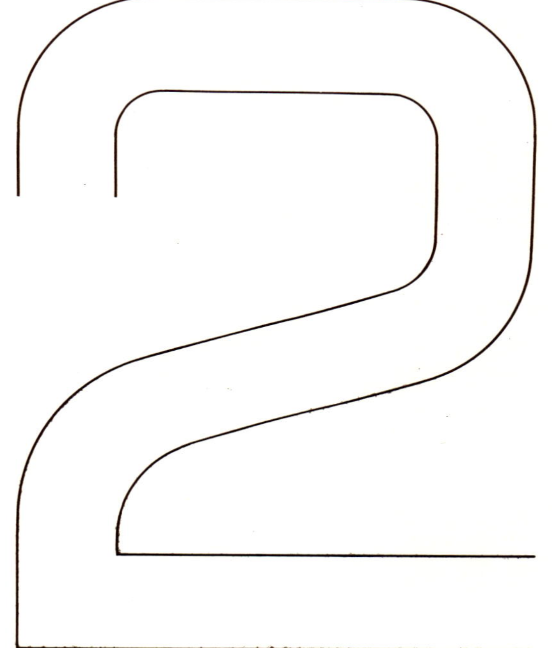

NOONTIDE

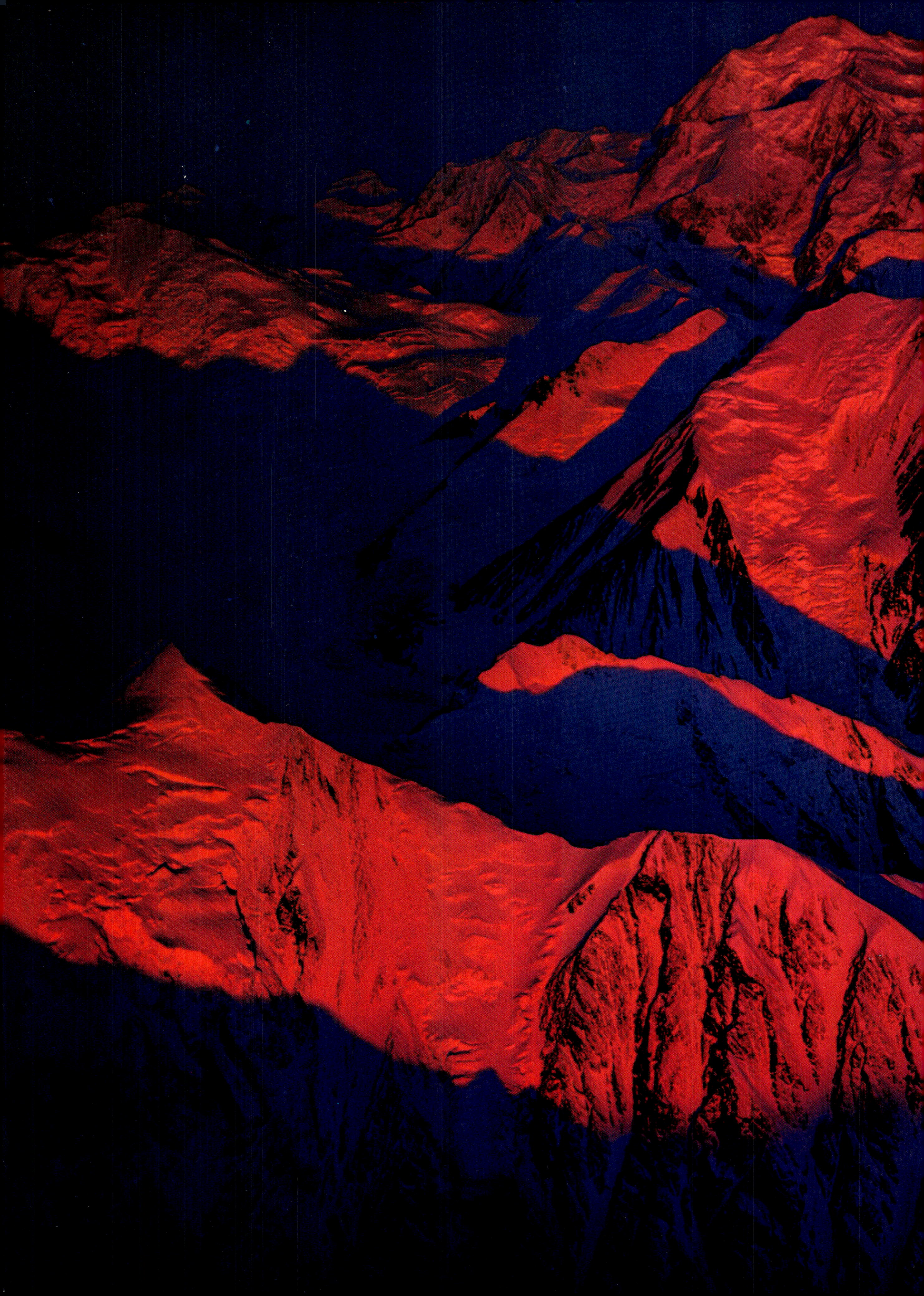

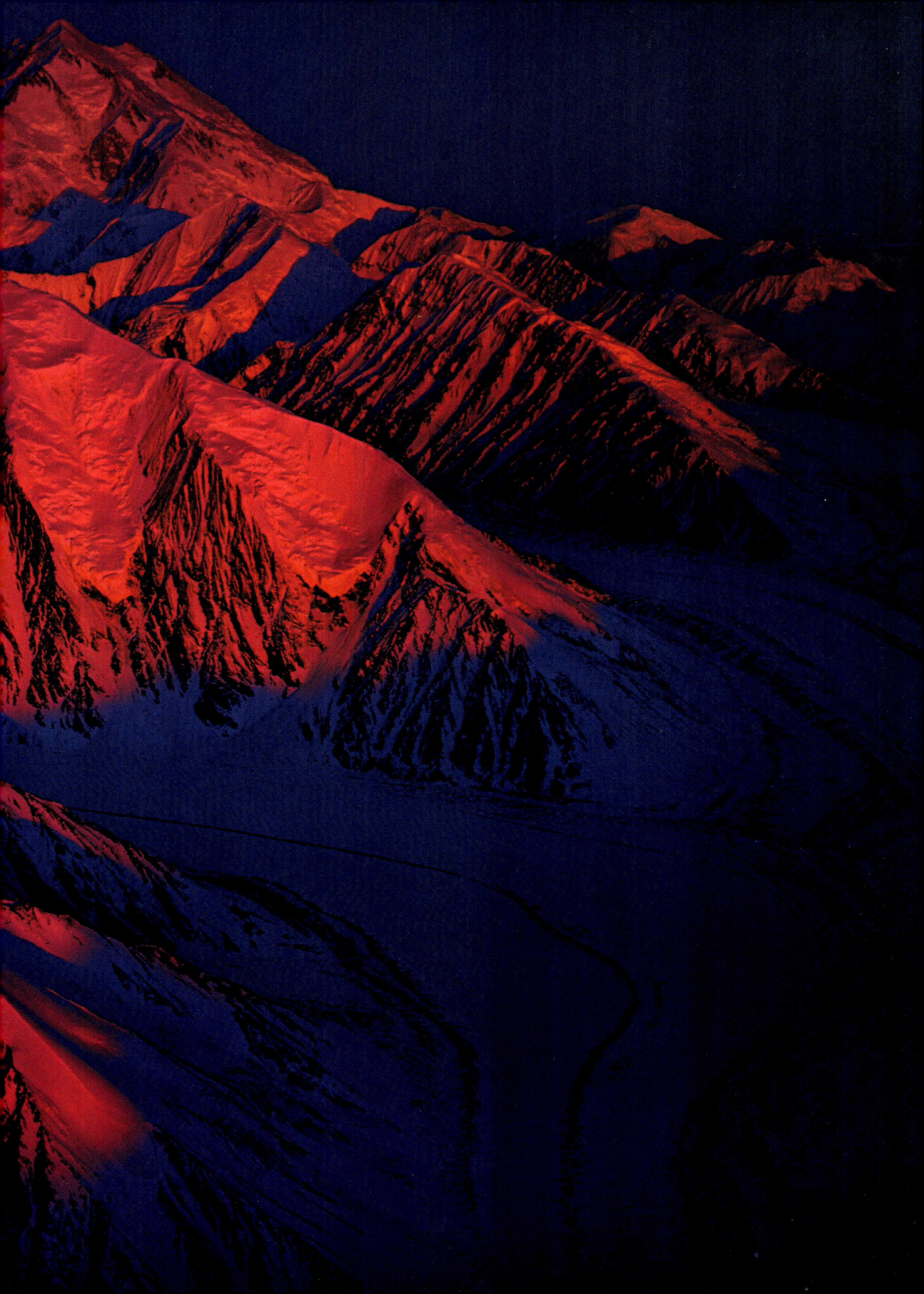

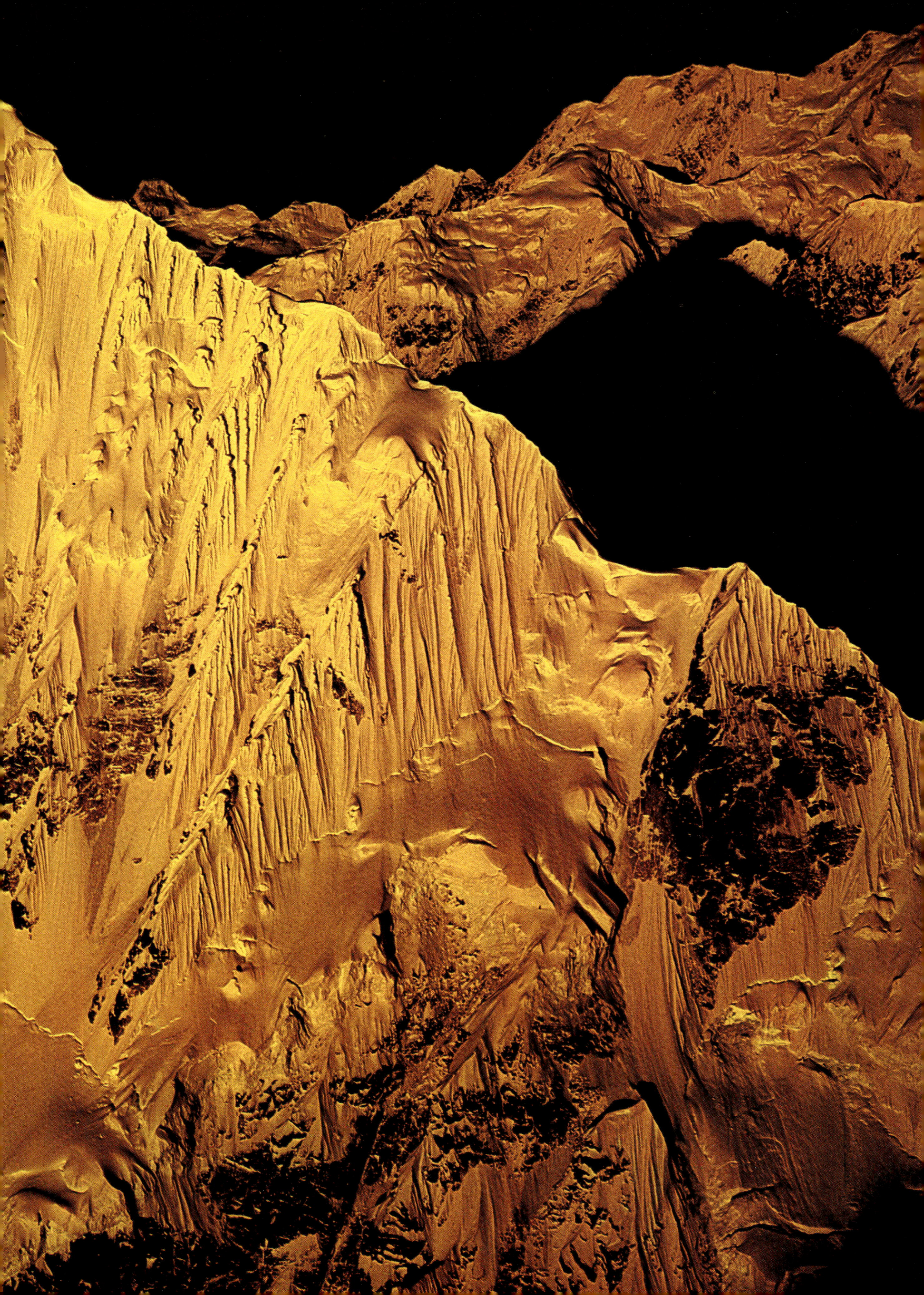

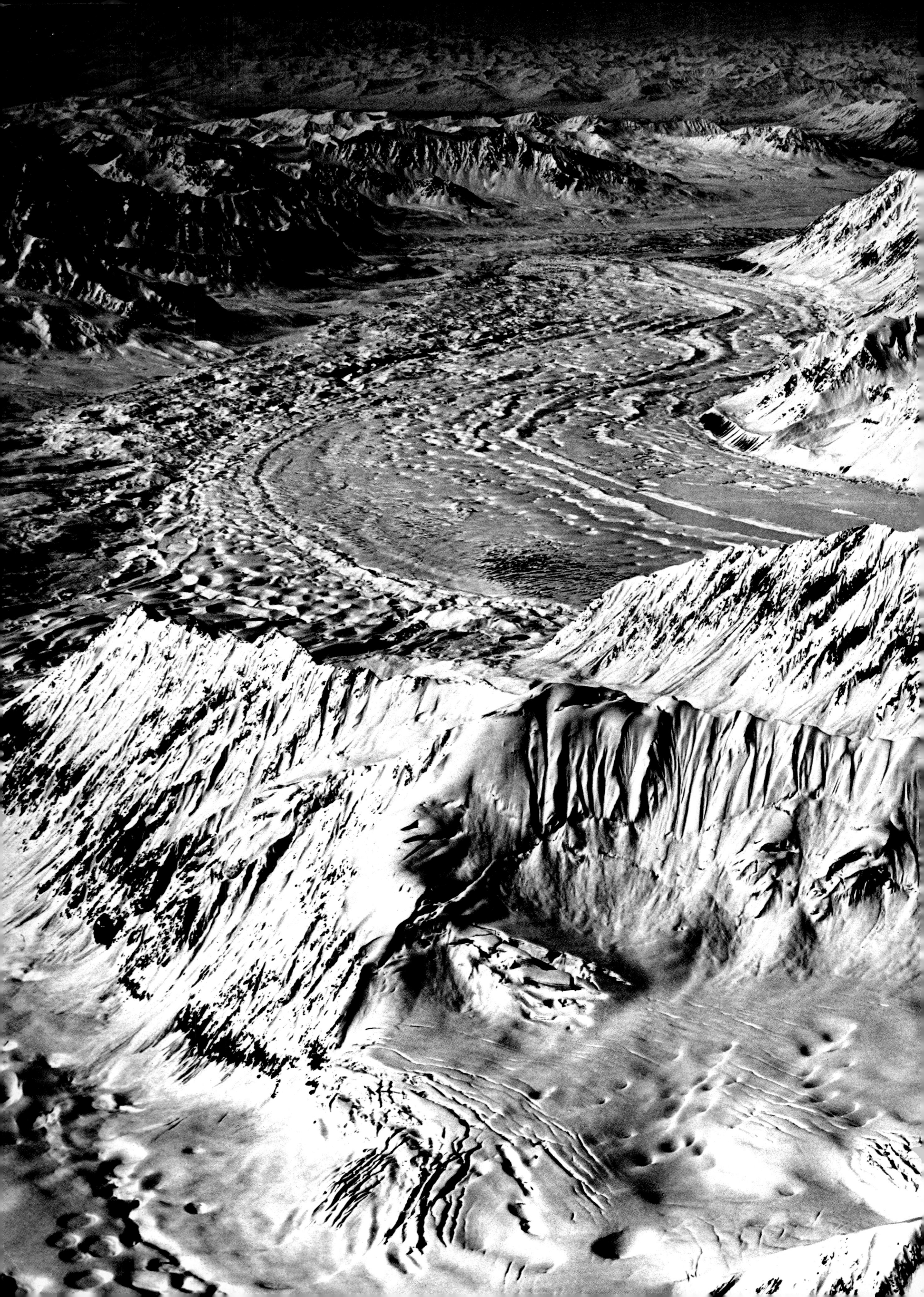

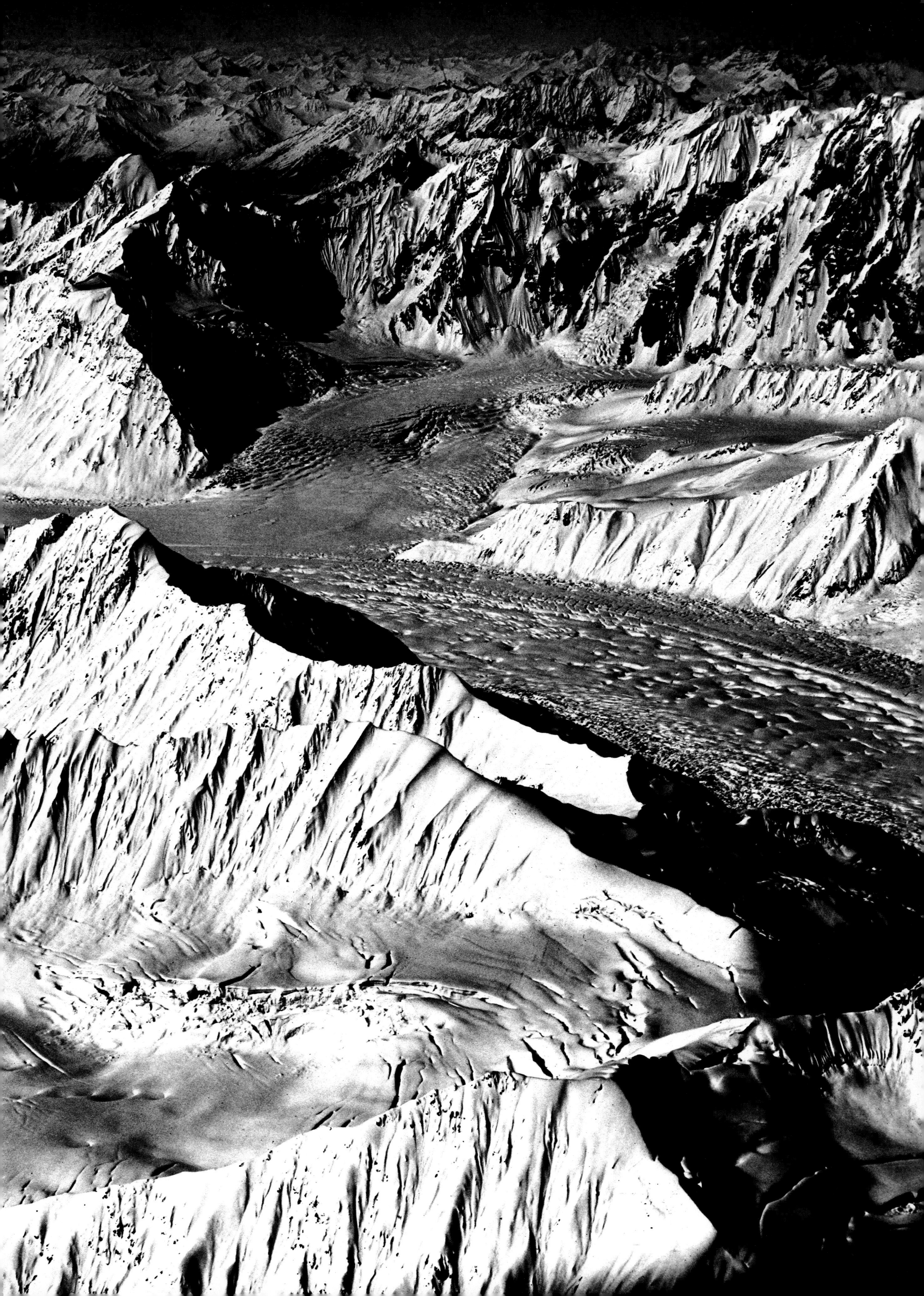

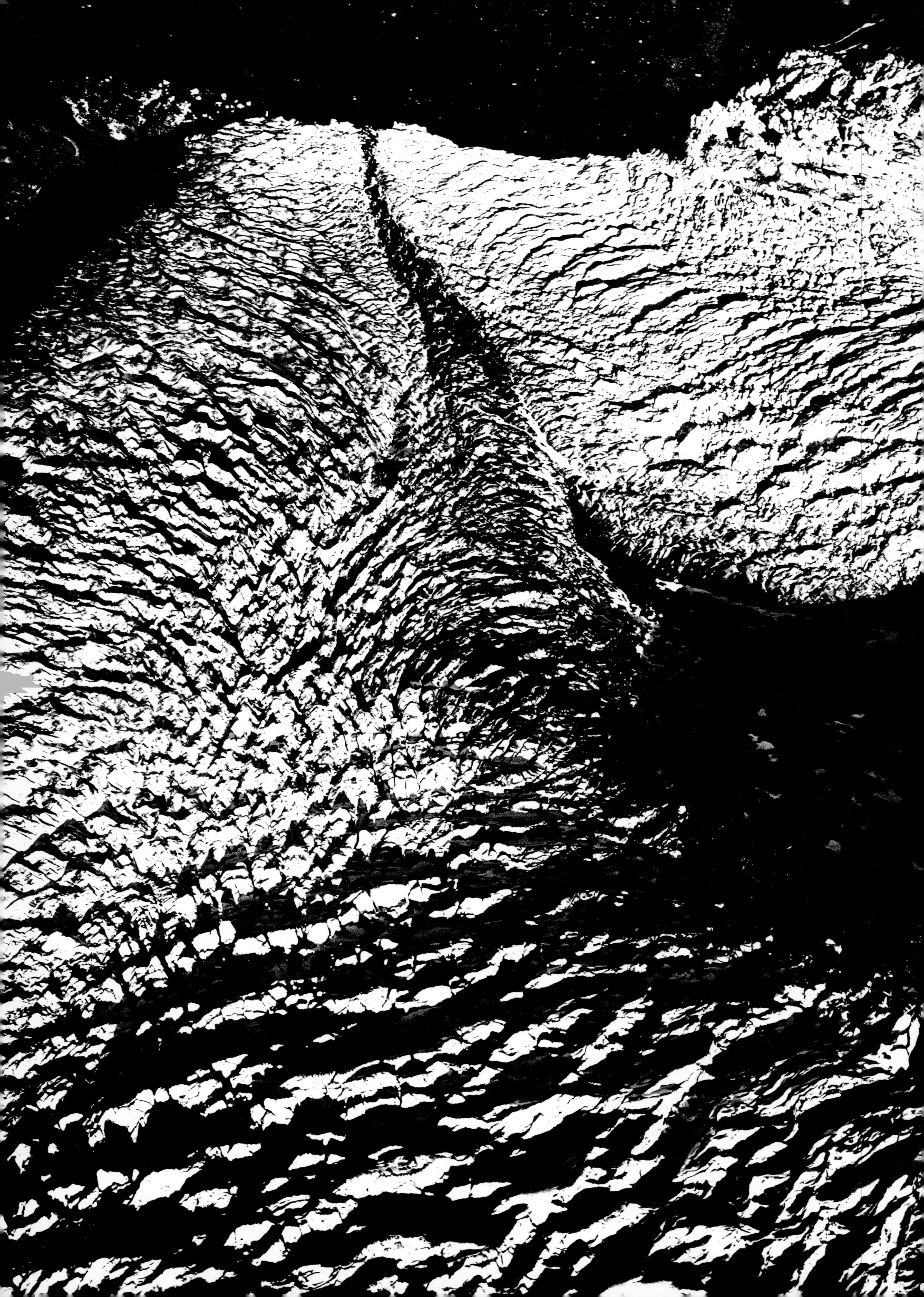

Prior to 1970, I spent nearly four years in seven countries in and near the Himalayas, photographing the mountains from every angle and in all their moods. I finished that work in May of that year, and made my first visit to Alaska from June to August in 1971. The intervening year I had spent recuperating from my sojourn in the area known sometimes as the Roof of the World and sometimes as the Seat of the Gods. I had traveled nearly two thousand miles, often by tramping through the mountains, and not only was I tired but I had contracted one of the illnesses that man is heir to. This was probably attributable to my having often drunk the water of glaciers, which was muddy and contained—well, I know not what.

The weather around Mount McKinley during the summer of 1971 was especially bad; on only five days did the sun break through the overcast, and then for only a couple of hours or so in the morning. After Alaska, I had planned to continue my photography of America, but my health was still not good. It was then, after returning to Japan, that I contemplated my lifework in terms of man and the earth, nature and the human spirit.

I had been told that for taking pictures of Mount McKinley May would be the best month, so in May, 1973, I left Anchorage. The journey was an experience that I had not expected. Like my countrymen, and many foreigners, I had become used to the speed, convenience and comfort of the Japanese train known to foreigners as the "Bullet Train" and to the people who constructed it and constitute the majority of its passengers by a word that translates simply as the New Tokaido Line. The Alaskan Railroad train on which I traveled north to Talkeetna moved at a snail's pace, and the seats were very high. The trip lasted only half a day, but by the time I reached my destination, I was exhausted. It was a great relief to catch sight of the faces of Don Sheldon, who was to be my pilot, and Mrs. Powell, the manager of the hotel.

I spent about eighty hours in a Cessna piloted by Sheldon and came to know the lay of the mountains quite well. I began by sketching in my notebook the mountains and glaciers in which I was interested, and then he would take us there. Our day began at 3 A.M., if the weather was good, with one of my assistants waking up our pilot; after that we all went to the airport to make preparations for our flight.

Reaching our first objective, the northeastern side of Mount McKinley, took some time, because we could not fly at the same altitude all the way. Sometimes, the plane had to climb suddenly. After arriving we would wait for the contrast necessary for a good picture. The sign that the sun was rising over Muldrow Glacier was a dull glow, like that of a lamp, emitted by the summit of the mountain. The summit turned purple, but there was not enough contrast until, about four minutes later, it turned red. That was the moment, but only if the plane had been maneuvered into the proper position, which, needless to say, required considerable skill. With the opening of the window by the copilot's seat, the temperature inside the plane dropped drastically, but I continued my camera work as we circled.

After an hour of photographing McKinley's sunrise-tinted southern slope as we flew in a westerly direction, we returned to the airport. While the plane was being refueled, I reloaded my cameras. About an hour later, we took off again. It would then be around seven or eight o'clock in the morning, the best time for taking pictures of glaciers. Earlier than that, since they are located in deep valleys, they would be in deep shadow.

There are glaciers in the Alps and the Himalayas that I have taken many pictures of. Mount McKinley's are more beautiful. In the Alps, the glaciers tend to be small. Those of the

Himalayas are on a grand scale, but the ice is stained with mud, particularly in Nepal and particularly during the dry season (winter). There is little fresh snow during this season. At McKinley, with its characteristically inclement weather, mountains and glaciers are always mantled and beautiful with new snow.

The large glaciers on the south side of McKinley are, from east to west, Eldridge, Ruth, Togasitna, Kahiltna, Lacona and Yentna. Of these, only Kahiltna is not photogenic, being monotonous in its largeness. Nor is Mount McKinley an object of great interest to the photographer. Though I took no pictures, I once put on an oxygen mask and climbed to twenty-thousand feet to have a look at North America's highest peak. I believe the best pictures of McKinley are taken from afar and include its neighbors.

Mount Huntington, to the east of McKinley, is much more suitable for the camera, especially the northeast wall. Rising a little more than twelve thousand feet, it is not a large mountain, but it is comparable to those in the Himalayas in the twenty-three-thousand-foot range.

When we flew to the north side of McKinley, we found rivers to photograph. The only large glacier is Muldrow, but from the small glaciers, rivers of great beauty flow like lacework through the tundra. Whether from the ground or from the air, good pictures of rivers are difficult to obtain, but here it was different. The rivers wend their way through forests, their flood-swollen waters often tearing up vast tracts; smaller streams find their way into larger streams in a delicate pattern. It was a scene to stir the enthusiasm of any photographer.

From the peaks and glaciers of the Alaska Range, we went on to the wind- and rain-swept panhandle of Alaska. We took a bus from the small airport at Gustavus to Glacier Bay Lodge at Bartlett Cove, where I was surprised to find an excellent hotel, for all around was only the desolate scene of sea, mountains and ice. I was even more surprised to find at the entrance to the lodge a large piece of paper on which was written in Japanese "Welcome Mr. Shirakawa." There were so few people that the place might be classified as uninhabited, but there was not only my name but it was written in Japanese.

The writer turned out to be an American by the name of Elder Kenneth, who had been trying to spread the Mormon faith among the Japanese in the port city of Kobe. He had been staying at the lodge for a few days and had learned about my visit from the park service. We got together with him several times, and I must say that he took good care of us during our ten-day stay.

Alaska, as everyone knows, is big. It is four times larger than Japan, but even in terms of the United States, it comprises one-sixth of the total area of the fifty states. And Glacier Bay National Monument, the largest of all the national parks, is big too, having an area three-fifths the size of the island of Shikoku, where my home prefecture is located.

There are no roads. When I asked park rangers about this, I learned that I would have to take all my pictures either from the sea or from the air. Which way to go, I decided, would depend on the weather. Fine days, if there were any, would be good for aerial photography, and on days of cloudiness, I would take to the sea.

The shape of the park resembles that of a clenched fist, the western side facing the Pacific Ocean and Glacier Bay dividing it into east and west all the way north to the border with Canada. I followed my usual practice of rising early and began taking pictures at 4:30 in the morning. Since snow is abundant, the glaciers are beautiful, like those of Mount McKinley.

During the time of day that was night in lower latitudes but here only evening—9:30 to

11:30 P.M.—we flew over the sea and took pictures of La Perouse Glacier, whose snout is the only one in the world to rise directly above the Pacific Ocean. Glaciers, unlike volcanoes, never put on a mask of dormancy, and the ones in this area are noticeably in a state of retreat. The whole of Glacier Bay was a basin filled with an ice sheet as recently as two and one half centuries ago. And less than twenty years ago, in 1958, occurred one of those cataclysmic events that so awe with the power of the forces unleashed. The cause was an earthquake and the result was devastation; in a short time, millions of tons of earth crashed down the mountain and tore loose hundreds of feet of Lituya Glacier. The wave created crested at one-third of a mile in height, collided with North Crillon Glacier across an arm of the bay, and swept eight miles southwestward to the mouth of the bay, leaving an uprooted forest in its wake. The havoc can be seen today.

We returned by crossing over Brady Icefield and viewed the moon rising over Glacier Bay to the southeast. Several days later we took a National Park Service motorboat about sixty miles up the bay to see Grand Pacific and other glaciers. In Johns Hopkins Inlet, we were caught in a great rainstorm. The wind from the mountains was pushing the icebergs through the mile-wide mouth of the inlet. It was a spectacular sight, but we were not without fear, for the icebergs could easily crush our small boat.

There were also waves, big and dangerous, which kept our boat at a distance of one to two miles from Margerie Glacier, whose wall of ice looms one hundred feet above the inlet. Even at that distance, the waves rocked our boat, as, continually cracking and booming, monstrous chunks of ice left the land and joined the sea. To our right, Grand Pacific Glacier was also calving. What a sight! I was fascinated and felt I would never tire of watching this, one of nature's spontaneous dramas.

The catacylism that created Crater Lake in Oregon took place nearly seven centuries ago. What happened to Mount Mazama (at twelve thousand feet about the same height as Mount Fuji) is not known with certainty, but it is believed that the volcano first erupted and then collapsed inward. In any case, there is now rain-fed and snow-fed Crater Lake. The lakes in this world are countable, but their number is very great. I know that I have never seen a more beautiful lake anywhere, especially when viewed from the top of the Watchman, a sheer-sided portion of the crater wall that rises eighteen hundred feet above the surface of the lake.

I took photographs from the air several times, putting on an oxygen mask and climbing to an altitude of twenty thousand feet in order to be able to include the whole lake. These pictures were not very successful, however, for they reminded me only of a pond in a small Japanese garden.

One day we spent the whole day driving the thirty-three miles around the lake, the seventh deepest freshwater lake in the world. The floor of this caldera, 1,932 feet below the surface, is thought to be flat, and a number of volcanic cones formed at a later period rise from the floor. Two of them, Wizard Island and Phantom Ship, break the deep blue surface. It was the middle of August and the sun was hot, but the average altitude is 6,600 feet and we did not feel the heat too much.

There is one path that leads down to the lake, to Cleetwood Cove, and from there a park service boat goes back and forth to Wizard Island four or five times a day. It was a surprise to be told that it carried only a handful of tourists each trip; in Japan, I imagined that there would be many more trips each day and the boat would be full each time.

For eighteen days in May and early June, we had visited the wilderness of Katmai National Park on the Alaska Peninsula, staying at the village of King Salmon and being subject to exorbitant rates at a hotel that was really nothing more than a barracks—two narrow beds in a small room. There was no other place to stay and no roads leading to another town or village. In the park itself, there were no roads, there were no trails, there were not even any paths. And the weather was stormy, windy and foggy; the sun pierced the overcast for only a few hours during those two and one half weeks.

Deep emerald green and never freezing because of its sulphur content, Katmai Crater Lake lies among volcanoes. As in the Himalayas, I had to fly or trudge through the snow. Light was the problem. There was enough to reveal the shapes of the mountains, but shape alone is nonsense. The pictures I wanted had to show the splendor of nature and also had to express my appreciation of it. Light was not enough; I needed the rays of the sun.

No one was there, apparently no one witnessed it, but the earth erupted stupendously at Katmai in 1912. Here too, the event has to be reconstructed ex post facto. It seems that molten lava drained through conduits from Mount Katmai to Mount Novarupta, six miles away. Then Novarupta exploded and Katmai collapsed. Hundreds of thousands of cubic yards of volcanic ash were lifted into the atmosphere, darkening skies and lowering temperatures throughout the Northern Hemisphere. Under seven hundred feet of ash, the trees of the valley were carbonized, and from thousands of holes bubbled gas and water vapor, giving rise to the name Valley of Ten Thousand Smokes.

I took pictures of other lakes, high in the Rocky Mountains. I had once seen a photograph of a lake on an airline poster and decided that I would visit it someday. This was Saint Mary Lake in Glacier National Park, Montana. This is a typical mountain lake, but my purpose in traveling thousands of miles from region to region was not to take ordinary snapshots. So here I did my camera work early in the morning, late in the evening or when it was stormy. It was the middle of August; summer is the only suitable season, for only until then does the rising sun cast red rays on the lake. When I returned in September, the high mountains obstructed the sun, and I could take no good pictures.

To get there, we crossed the Continental Divide from west to east by taking the Going to the Sun road through Logan Pass. During my travels in the United States, I camped at almost all of the national parks and monuments I visited. The one at Saint Mary Lake, in the middle of the forest, was the best—so wide that we could not see other campers. There was, not for the first time, the great temptation to set up camp and stay for several weeks.

The national park campsites were all wonderful. Where visitors were numerous, the camping grounds were equipped with such conveniences as showers, washing machines and automatic dryers. And the number of people employed to take care of nature was quite large. I understand that the number of national park rangers is seven thousand, and during the summer this number is temporarily increased by five- or six-fold.

The roads, the excellent facilities for campers and the great number of rangers led me to some comparisons with my own country and reflections on ways of protecting nature, which seems to have been regarded by many as infinitely expendable. In my own country, there are less than one hundred people taking care of the national parks, and in many places, the landscape has been scarred by mundane constructions, such as golf courses. In America, I understand the problem has been with loggers, ranchers and extractors of the wealth of the earth. Such things upset nature's balance.

In America I found encouraging signs. The Going to the Sun road was cut through solid rock, but care was taken not to offend nature. Yellowstone was the first national park in the world, and in only a century some of the resistance to taking active steps to preserve nature has been overcome. This is by no means the whole story or the end of the story. Nevertheless, I wondered if the young republic was not being more successful than my own centuries-old culture.

Noontide

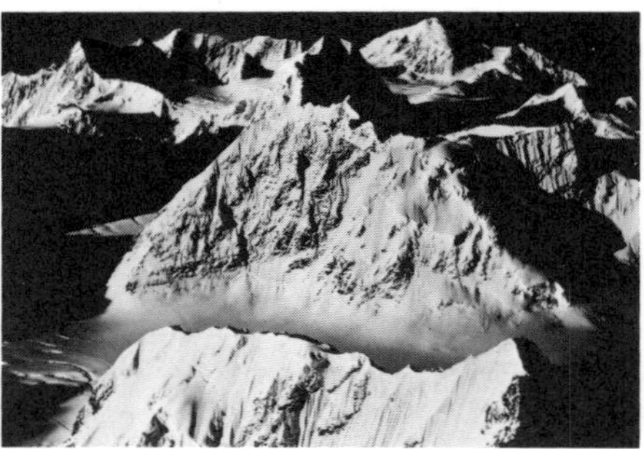

Fairweather Mountain
Glacier Bay National Monument has an area of 4,381 square miles and is the largest national park in the United States. Fairweather Mountain (15,300 feet) is the highest peak in the park. It is seen in the upper right of this picture taken in the early morning directly from the north. The Fairweather Range is a spur of the Saint Elias Mountains on the U.S.-Canada border. I do not know which country we were over; I do know that flying over rugged mountains and deep valleys in a light plane equipped only with pontoons is a harrowing experience.

Mount McKinley
The South Peak of Mount McKinley (upper left) is the highest point in North America (20,300 feet). The North Peak, to the right, is 19,470 feet. In front of these, Mount Tatum is actually lower than Mount Brooks, only the crest of which catches the dawning sun (11,140 and 11,936 feet). On the right is Muldrow Glacier, the main part of which is between Mount McKinley and Mount Tatum. Flowing from between Mount Tatum and Mount Brooks is Traelika Glacier. These glaciers flow north, but most of Mount McKinley's large glaciers flow to the south.

Northeast Wall of Mount Huntington
Among the one hundred most famous mountains of the world, because of its form, is Mount Huntington (12,234 feet). Its fame comes from the sheer east wall (actually northeast), which looks as if it had received a blow from a gargantuan sword. Facing this wall are four mountains over 11,000 feet in height. To capture the golden, early light of morning, we flew between the mountains. Below us, flowing from right to left at this point, was West Fork Ruth Glacier. These mountains and glaciers in the Alaska Range are in Mount McKinley National Park.

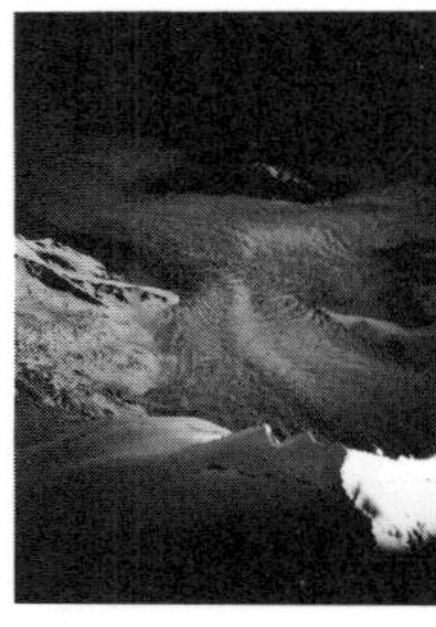

La Perouse Glacier
Although pictures taken from the sea were equally as dramatic, I prefer this one taken from the mid slope of Mount La Perouse (10,728 feet). Flowing toward the upper left, the ice forms a sheer cliff and plunges directly into the Pacific Ocean (the only glacier to do so). Reflected are the rays of the setting sun and the blue of the sky. Fifteen miles to the northwest, an earthquake in 1958 sent 90 million tons of rock and 1,000 feet of Lituya Glacier into Lituya Bay, creating a wave 1,720 feet high. On its way to the ocean, the wave uprooted a whole forest.

Wizard Island
About 6,600 years ago, in what is now the State of Oregon, lava flowed out of fissures in the mountain, and the peak of 12,000-foot Mount Mazama collapsed inward, forming a basin that became a lake. Pumice carried by the wind eighty miles to the northeast suggests that an explosion preceded the collapse. Wizard Island, rising 760 feet above Crater Lake, is the cinder cone of a volcano formed at a later date. Taking off from Klamath Falls Airport before dawn, we photographed the lake and the sunrise. This picture is taken from the east.

Katmai Crater Lake
From the middle of May to early June, we stayed at the village of King Salmon, Alaska, but the sky cleared on only one of the eighteen days we were there, and then for only two hours. Moisture coming in from the Pacific Ocean condenses when it meets the cold air over the glaciers, so it is foggy and cloudy throughout the year. In this photograph taken around 11 A.M. from a plane flying west of Mount Katmai, a cloud cover obscures Mount Trident and other volcanoes in the vicinity. This is the Aleutian Range on the Alaska Peninsula.

Saint Mary Lake I
Canada and the United States established the Waterton-Glacier
International Peace Park in 1932. This photograph of Saint
Mary Lake in Montana was taken in the middle of August, on
the first of our two visits. This is the only time of year when the
mountains are full of color; by my second visit at the end of
September, the flowers of summer were gone. In the middle of
the lake is Goose Island. In the distance, the mountain in the
center is Mount Reynolds (9,157 feet); to the left are Mount
Citadel and Mount Little Chief.

Saint Mary Lake II
As the weather changes, mountains change, especially at high
altitudes. Although it was mid August when I took this picture,
a strong wind, bitterly cold, was blowing through Logan Pass
on the Continental Divide, ruffling the surface of the lake.
Mount Reynolds is hidden by clouds. In the center is Mount
Little Chief (9,548 feet); these peaks are in the Lewis Range.
The stone of the mountains was formed by the hardening of
sand and lime, once covered by a vast sea. Major highways run
through Glacier National Park's 1,583 square miles.

Crater Lake and Setting Sun
This lake was discovered by the explorer John Wesley Hillman
in 1853. He called it Deep Blue Lake, while later "discoverers"
called it Blue Lake, Lake Majesty and Crater Lake. The highest
point in the crater, a little over 8,000 feet, is Hillman Peak,
seen at the right. Eighteen hundred feet above the lake is the
Watchman, seen at the left. From there the view of Crater Lake
National Park and southwestern Oregon is superb. One can
walk up from the parking lot, and the distance is less than one
mile. Several volcanic cones rise from the floor of the caldera.

black & white plates

Upper Reaches of Lacona Glacier
The glaciers on the northern side of Mount McKinley are small
and short and soon turn into rivers. Lacona Glacier is one of
the larger ones on the southern side and is directly east of
Yentna Glacier, which is the largest on the western side. Lacona
does not have the bright look of other glaciers; rather it seems
to be always in a brooding mood. From the air, the ice, though
it gave the feeling of great coldness, appeared yellowish, due to
the fact that there was little snow on the surface. The dark
circles on the surface of the glacier are ponds.

Lower Reaches of Lacona Glacier
From our base at Talkeetna, we always began our photography
of Mount McKinley from the eastern side in the early morning
and then went on to the southern side. On our return, we always passed over Kahiltna and Lacona glaciers. Flowing from
the southern slopes of Mount Foraker, the latter broadens
considerably in its lower reaches. We followed this route scores
of times, the very best times being in the month of May. After
June, without their cover of snow, the mountains near the lower
part of the glacier look disfigured and dilapidated.

Yentna Glacier Dividing
The wide line running perpendicularly is a medial moraine, the
predominant colors of which are yellow and deep blue. Using
color film, I took special care to catch the colors. Monochrome
film, depending on the angle, is even more effective than color
film for reproducing the delicate texture of the moraine and
brings out features that cannot be seen with the naked eye. This
photograph was taken on the western side of Mount McKinley.
We flew among high mountains lying to the front, to the left
and to the right. Glacier ice may be thousands of feet thick.

Crumbling Margerie Glacier

In Tarr Inlet, we stopped our boat for about four hours and watched the spectacle of this glacier calving. To our right, Grand Pacific Glacier was also calving. It was like a competition. It had been raining, sometimes heavily, and I wondered if that hastened the breaking off of the ice. Photography was difficult; not only did we lack a firm foothold but being two miles away, it took the sound ten seconds to reach us. To the left is a lone seagull in flight. I took this picture around seven in the evening (Glacier Bay National Monument).

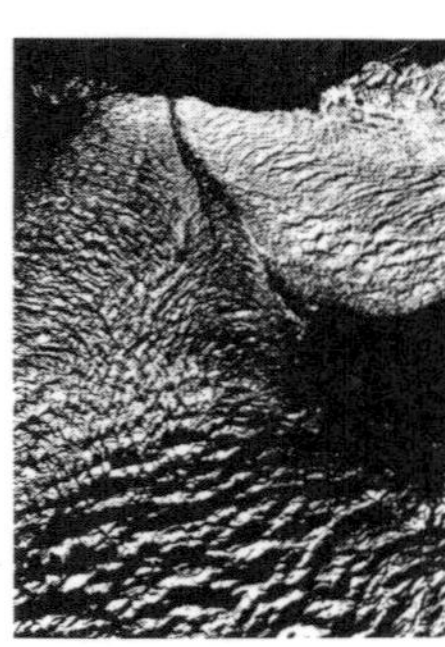

Riggs Glacier

Riggs Glacier is to the east of Muir Glacier at the northern end of Muir Inlet, a twenty-mile-long arm of Glacier Bay. This photograph was taken from the air in the early morning. Glaciers here are retreating at an unusually rapid pace. In 1794, when Captain George Vancouver navigated the Icy Strait, the depression that is now Glacier Bay was filled with an ice sheet extending more than 100 miles to the Saint Elias Range. From the mouth of the bay to Grand Pacific Glacier is now a journey of 65 miles. Care is necessary to avoid the floating ice.

Wizard Island and Mount Scott

Although it looks flat, Mount Scott, seen to the left, has two peaks. I took this photograph from the entrance to the trail leading to the top of the Watchman (Crater Lake National Park). The sun was low on the horizon, and in the light of dusk, the shoreline lurked in the fusion of the walls of the crater and the deep blue waters of the lake. In the foreground, flowers whose roots are in volcanic ash are tiny but appear large because they are only two and one half feet from the lens. Wizard Island rises one half mile from the bottom of the lake.

Crater Lake

The weather was good every day during our one-week stay in the middle of August. The last day was windless and particularly splendid. On the morning when this photograph was taken from near Pumice Point, the deep blue surface of the lake was as smooth as a mirror. We were looking to the south. To the left is Chaski Bay, and the looming, black mountain is Applegate (8,135 feet). What appears as a black round mass to the left is Phantom Ship, a volcanic cone. In the middle is Eagle Point, looking more like a monkey than its eponym.

Bird's-eye View of Crater Lake

We boarded a Cessna and took off early in the morning to photograph Crater Lake National Park, the highest peak in which, seen in the upper part of the picture, is Mount Scott (8,926). The lava walls around Crater Lake rise 500 to 2,000 feet above the surface. The deepest part of the lake, ascertained by sonar soundings, is 1,932 feet below the reflection of the sunlight. Running clockwise around the lake is a one-way road thirty-three miles long; there are more than twenty observation platforms. We spent a whole day driving around the lake.

Lake Grinnell

This is in the middle of Glacier National Park, but scenery like this greets the eye as soon as one enters the park. One route between Great Falls, Montana (to the southeast), and Calgary, Alberta (to the north), goes through the park. A century ago, explorers were seeking a pass through the Rocky Mountains. The falls reflected in Grinnell Lake are Grinnell Falls. The glacier to the left is Grinnell, and above that, looking like a shelf, is Salamander Glacier. The mountains above are called Garden Wall; the biggest one on the left is Angel Wing.

View from Cloudcap

There is a place where Rim Drive, which circles Crater Lake, curves away from the edge of the lake to bypass Mount Cloudcap. There is also a small road that goes directly to Cloudcap Bay. The view from there is a majestic panorama. It is estimated that the collapse of Mount Mazama destroyed seventeen cubic miles of the volcano. Although the lake has no outlet, the water that fills the caldera about halfway comes entirely from rain and snow and is not saline. Wizard Island is seen in the distance, and beyond that are the Watchman and Hillman Peak.

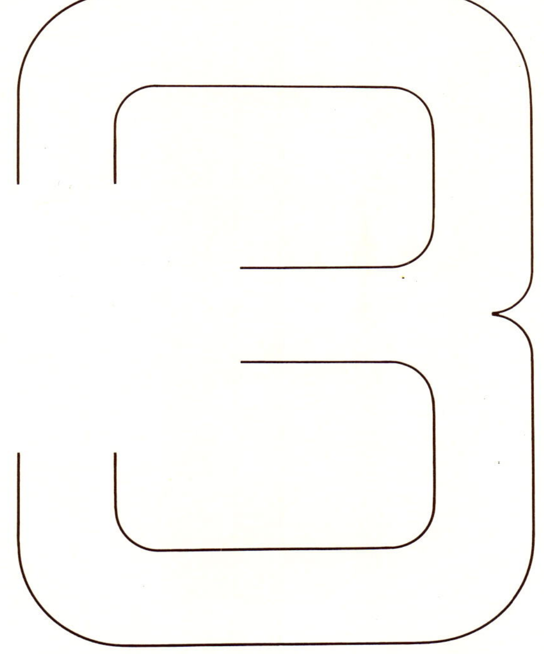

EVENTIDE

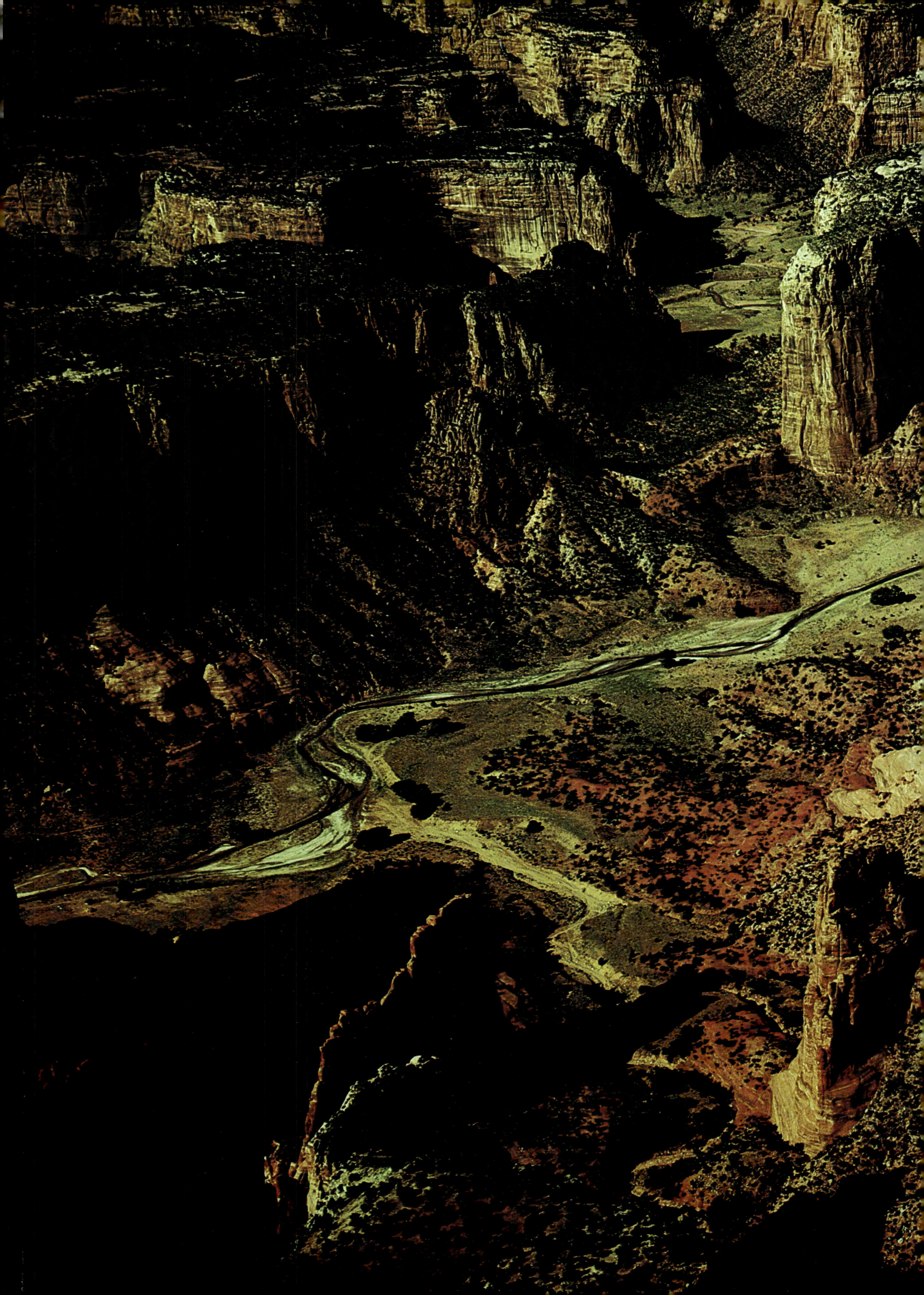

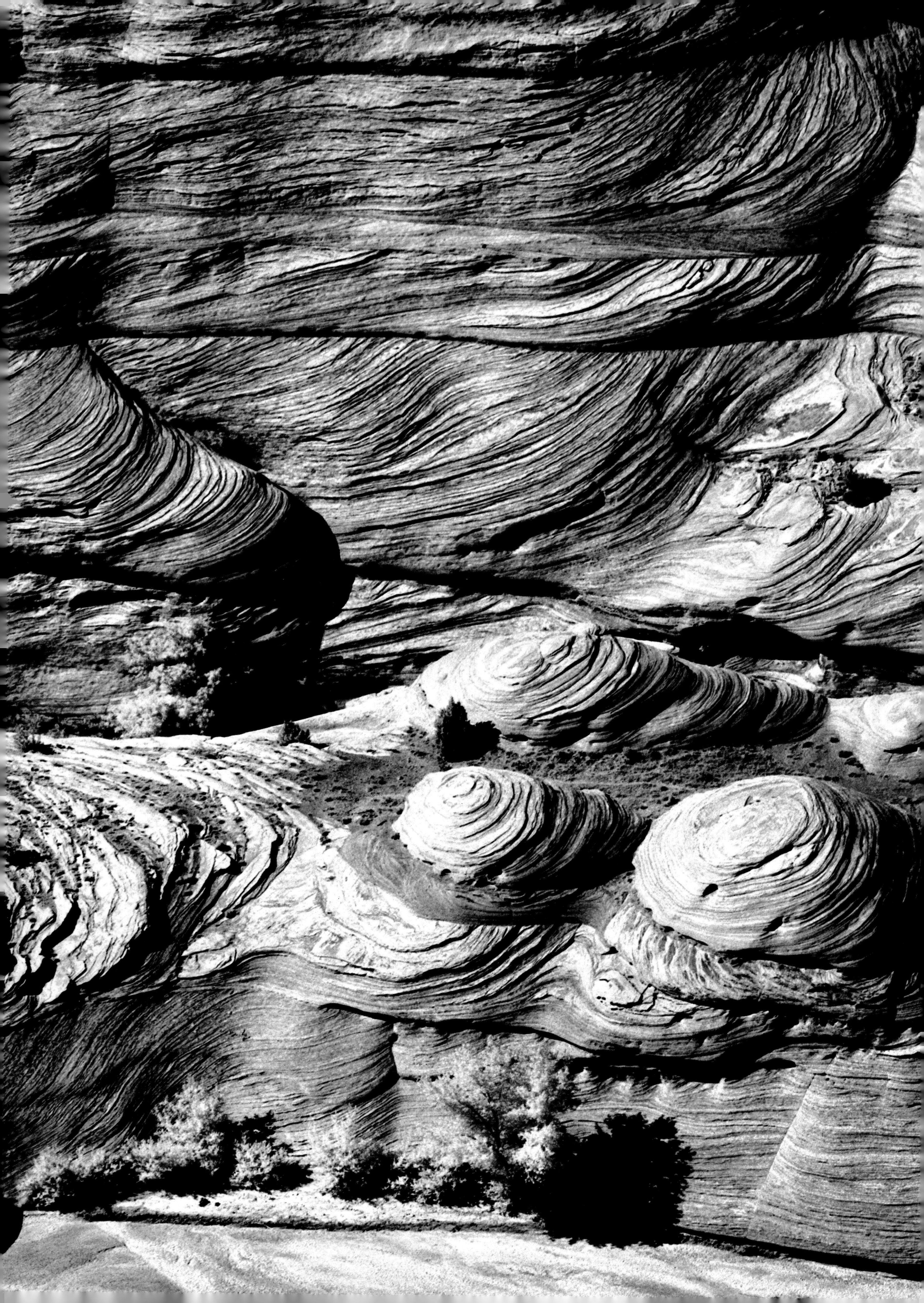

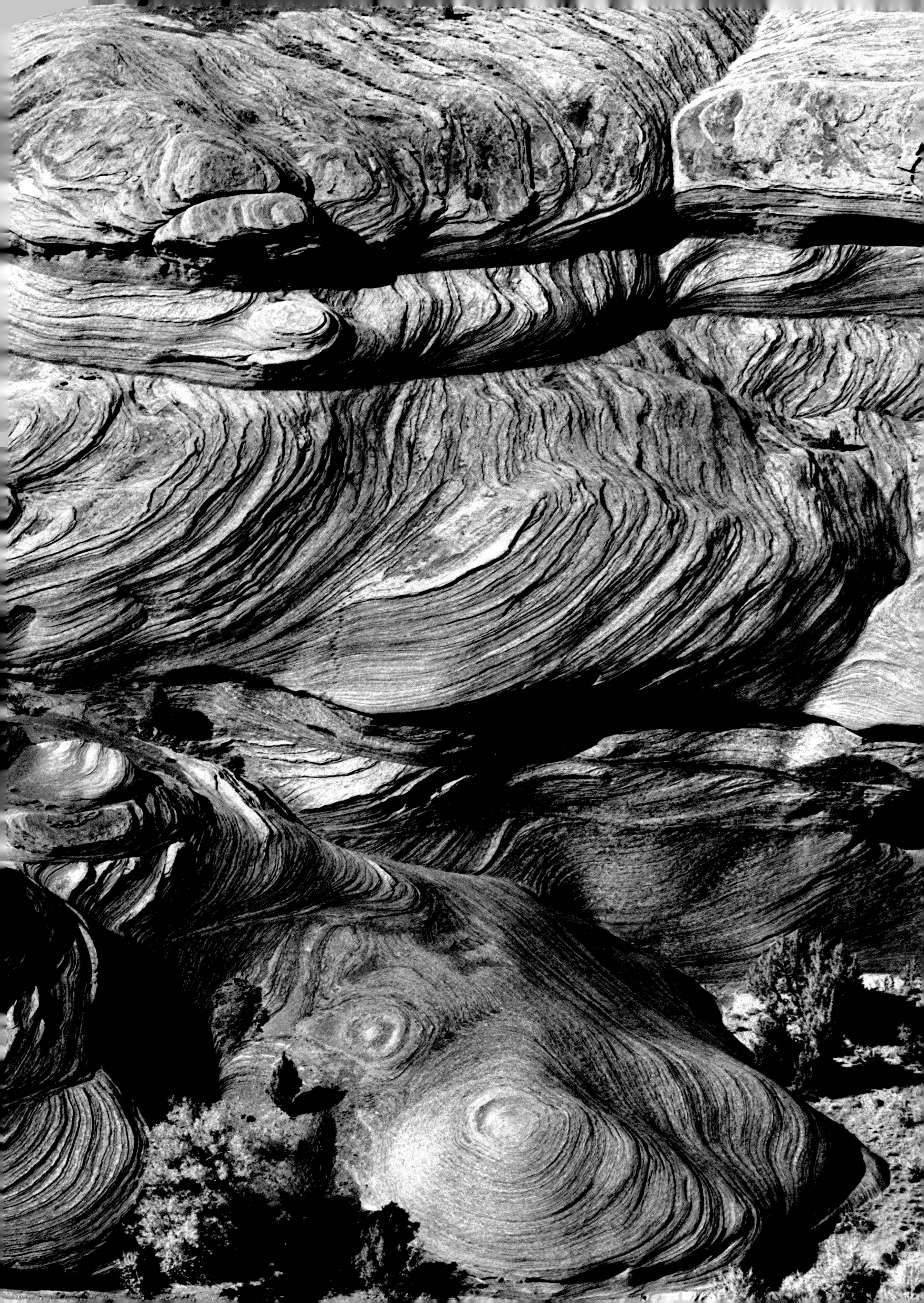

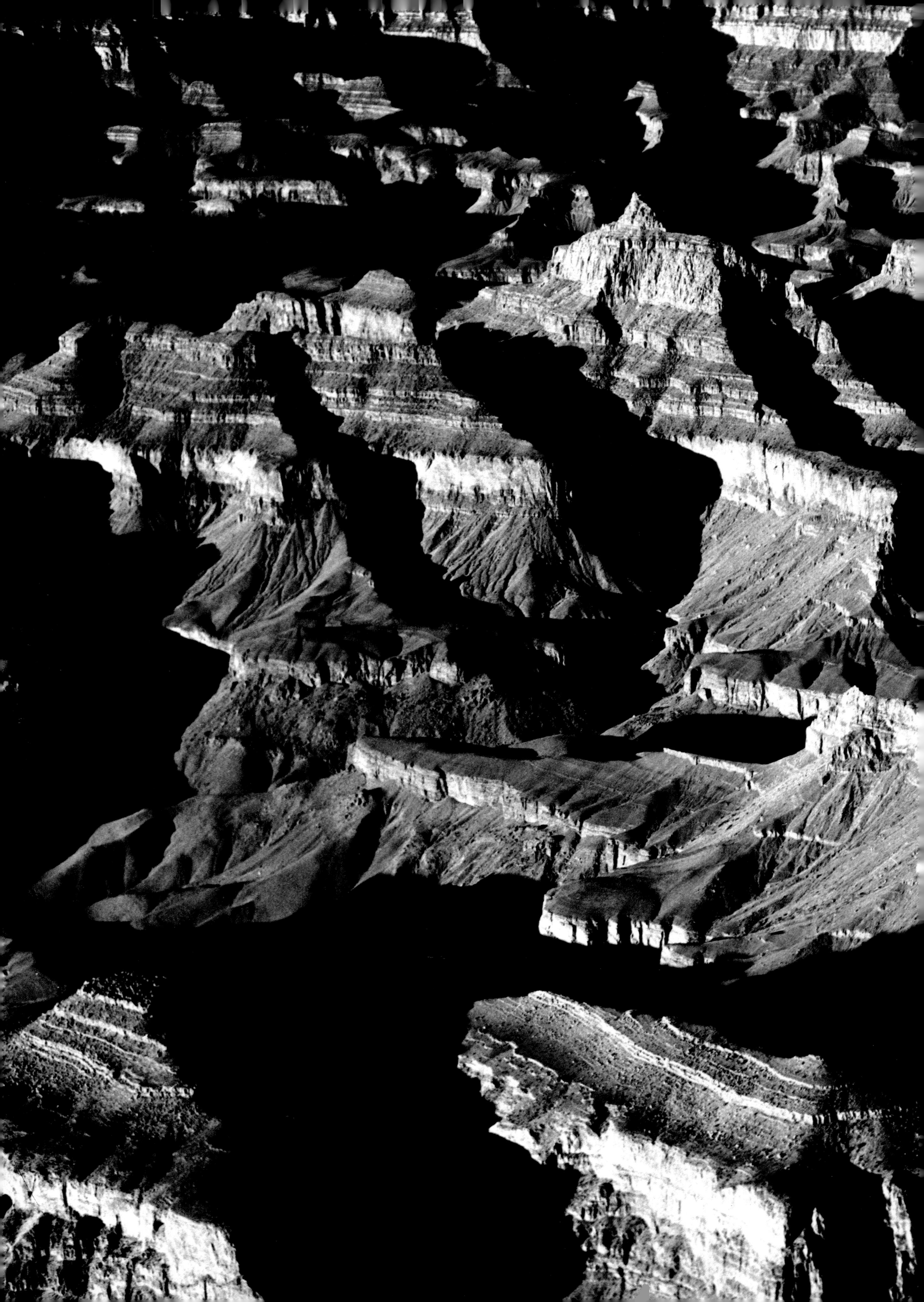

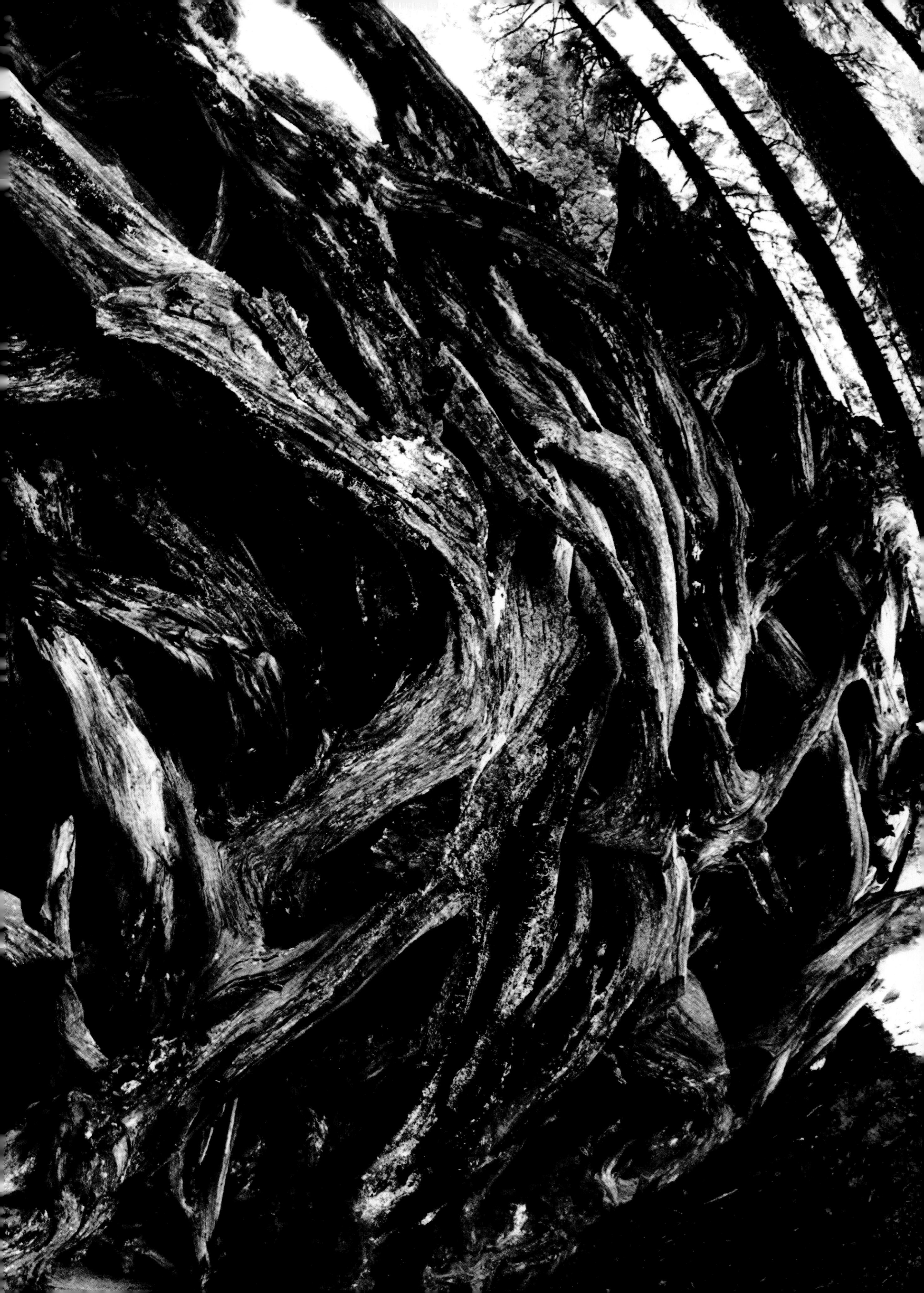

March 13 was the date we left the Petrified Forest National Park and set out for the Grand Canyon. The first leg of our drive was fine, very pleasant. When we reached Winslow, Arizona, it began to snow heavily, and in the twenty-five miles from Flagstaff to Williams, we passed only one car going in the opposite direction.

As the wind whipped the sides of the camper and snow froze on the windshield, we could barely see our way ahead, and our pace was slowed to that of a turtle. We debated whether to go on, but I wanted desperately to photograph the canyon in a snowstorm. Since we had enough supplies for several days, we could, if necessary, set up camp. We decided to risk it. It would be much better than being stranded in the Himalayas, I thought.

After we turned north at Williams, the severity of the storm lessened, but it was already evening before we reached the snowy gates of the park. We had covered less than two hundred miles. No one was at the gate; our camper slid left and right as we inched our way to the park office on the South Rim. Waiting to greet us was Merle E. Stitt, the park superintendent. After warm handshakes, we managed to breathe a sigh of relief.

In fact, everywhere we went the National Park Service people welcomed us warmly, accorded us the kindest hospitality, and cooperated graciously. We were extremely grateful for this, though at other times the condition of the society itself gave me pause for thought. While the grandeur of nature in the United States remains the best in the world, one wonders whether the society itself is healthy.

In publishing this book, I have pondered deeply on that land to which I went as a visitor. The questions are difficult. For example, does not the sad tale of white man versus aborigine or man of any other color, of good guys versus bad guys a la the Western movie strongly suggest that racial discrimination transcends any philosophy of the people and has become their blood, flesh and bones? And what psychology can lie behind the brutal slayings and mass murders, the precarious state of public safety that plagues particularly the cities? And the military might of the world's richest nation—many people in the world, even those who do not subscribe to the jingoish use of the word *genocide*, are appalled by brute force. Man's inhumanity to man may describe it, but it hardly explains it.

It is, perhaps, hardly good manners to point out the state of the emperor's attire, nor is America the only country to suffer from these and other problems, but in America the chasm between the lofty ideals of the beginning and the present condition remains so little narrowed.

Well, I digress. I have to hurry on to say that I was disappointed in my hope of having a picture of the Grand Canyon under snow. While there was deep snow on the rim, there was none in the mile-deep gorge. At the observation platform on the Kaibab Plateau, it is cold even in midsummer; on the banks of the Colorado River, deep in the canyon, it may be 110 degrees or hotter.

Thunder, rain, hail—in August I returned to take pictures of them. The storms of summer, which leave the desert white with hailstones for a few minutes, are incredible and indescribable, but strangely enough, snow does not fall in winter.

Usually from the North Rim, the thunderclouds would build and race toward us. In the darkness, a sudden cold, and then as if poured from giant ladles came the rain and sometimes hail. I used to take my pictures from the observation platform, but then we had to run for the car, for it would be only a matter of seconds until we were drenched to the skin. The rain centers are not so large, clouds seldom covering the whole canyon at one time, and before it all started the sky was clear.

During the spring and summer, good photography from the air was impossible because of turbulence. Pictures of the Grand Canyon number in the tens of thousands, but most are taken from the South Rim. Whether my efforts are artistic or not, I do not know; in any case I decided to follow the course of the canyon in the early morning from east, near Little Colorado, to west, near the Watchtower, and in the evening aim my camera eastward from Apache Point.

Our young pilot was a superb somersaulter. That, of course, is not for ordinary tourists, who also charter planes in great numbers. (This made it rather difficult for us to do so at the times important to us, but the park service was very obliging in making arrangements.) Around sunset, there were only forty seconds between our first and second shutter chance; we could not take advantage of this by circling. So it was up and over. Due to the removal of the door from our Cessna, care not to be flung out when we made a sharp turn was necessary. On one occasion, my seat belt came loose, which frightened not only me but my conscientious pilot.

I flew in and over the canyon scores of times, but always a strange thing happened. I could hear the strains of "Bali Hai." How it reached my ears—from the bottom of the canyon or from the cliffs, whether from someone's stereo or something else—I do not know. I had taken many, many aerial pictures of the American continent, but this was the first time that I heard "Bali Hai." Its source remains a mystery.

That summer of 1973 was very hot on the West Coast, with temperatures in Los Angeles rising above 100 degrees. Nevertheless, when we arrived from Kings Canyon, Yosemite Valley was full to overflowing. I had visited the park in the summer during the late fifties, but at that time there were few people and everything was quiet. This time, we stayed for only two days before moving on to pitch our tent near Bridalveil Fall. Had it been fall or winter, we would have selected a warm place under a large tree. In summer, we found that a cool place near the water and some rocks about twelve feet high was best.

One night an incident occurred that impressed me with the nearness of the wilderness. I always spent the night in the camper; my assistants slept in the tent. We retired early, and around ten o'clock I was stirred from my sleep by what sounded like a box falling from the table outside. This was followed by the sound of paper being torn. Wild dogs searching for food? I got out of the camper to investigate. In the darkness, half asleep, I came face to face with a bear no more than two yards away. I could have touched the beast, had I not been so frightened.

He took no notice of me, being intent on rummaging through our food supplies. Yelling to my assistants to be careful, I ran back to the camper, into which we all dived in no time at all.

We watched our unexpected and unheeding visitor through the darkness. After he emptied the boxes, he knocked the ice chest off the table. When it landed, the lid sprang open and out rolled our eggs, butter and soft drinks. We did not want the ice chest destroyed, so we shone a searchlight in his direction. Unfazed, he devoured the butter, making use of his huge tongue, and after punching a hole in the cans with his claws, went on to enjoy the Coca-cola and Seven-Up.

Exasperated after thirty minutes of this, we turned up our radio to full volume and leaned on our horn. He disappeared among the rocks, leisurely. Fearing that he might return, we gathered up the remnants of the food and burned them. And indeed, next morning we found more cans with holes punched in their sides. We felt rather shaken by one of nature's creatures.

In Yosemite Valley I had seen a comic sight. There was a large number of hippies, so large that they seemed to be the valley's sole occupants. Hair long and dirty and torsos bare, they often took advantage of the free rides offered on double-decker buses.

I was told that what they were against were established values and what they were for was living a life free of social fetters. They were to me, however, a strange sight. Could it really be that freedom lies in wearing one's hair long, or that a change in values comes from semi-nudity, or even nudity? To me it seemed more like a way of thinking common in Europe before the Reformation, according to which the purchase of indulgences was the way to heaven.

The hippies seldom go into the mountains; we saw none there. Perhaps their bared backs and chests prevent them from getting closer to the sun. During my four years in the Himalayas, I had not seen any either, though countries like India and Nepal are very popular with them. They prefer to congregate in cities, such as Kathmandu, and then principally in downtown districts. Contradictory as it may seem, this suggests that the freedom they advocate can be found only where large crowds congregate.

Several years ago in the United States, the lice that multiplied were traced to the dirty hair and beards of hippies. This was a matter of great concern to health authorities, because lice cause typhus. (I myself was caught in a typhus scare while photographing the Alps. It was not a pleasant experience.) Fortunately an extermination program was carried out, and there was no epidemic. It is obvious, at least to me, that there is merit in bathing and cleanliness, regardless of race, color, creed or length of hair.

Eventide

color plates

Bryce Canyon
In southern Utah, the formations in the southern half of Bryce Canyon National Park are called Pink Cliffs. The rocks in this vicinity, near the center of the park, are yellowish; when the rays of the rising sun fall on them, they turn a brilliant gold. This photograph was taken from Bryce Point. In the upper center, looking like a bay, is Silent City. Sunset Point, to the right, is 8,000 feet above sea level. Winding through the rocky peaks is a trail leading to Sunset Point and other places. Although it was then midsummer, early mornings were cold.

Canyon de Chelly
Tsegi, a Navajo word meaning "valley of rocks," is the source of this canyon's name. It came into English through Spanish and is pronounced *shey*. Canyon de Chelly National Monument is in northeastern Arizona, not far from the New Mexico border. Taken in the early morning from the north, this aerial picture shows the area where Canyon de Chelly and Monument Canyon meet. Spider Rock (804 feet) is at the upper right; to the left and above the rock can be seen the observation platform. The path leading there appears white among the trees.

White House
The Indians who now live in Canyon de Chelly are Navajos (the monument is part of the Navajo Indian Reservation), but this prehistoric stone dwelling was built by the Pueblos. Around 1300, they were driven from the valley by a prolonged drought. The high, white gypsum wall makes the site easy to pick out from a great distance and also explains the name. On the rock wall opposite White House, there is an observation platform. This picture, however, was taken about one mile downriver. Although it was April 2, the water was bone-chilling cold.

Bird's-eye View of the Grand Canyon I
On three visits in the winter, summer and fall, we took photographs from the air more than twenty times. The best time was in the fall, when the air currents were least turbulent and the colors were at their best. We were north of Comanche Point when we took this early morning picture in a westerly direction. In the foreground is Vishnu Temple, at right center is Wotan's Throne, and the two towers on the left are Angels Gate. The rocky peak in the upper center is Zoroaster Temple; the mesa to the right of it is Brahma Temple.

Salt Creek I
Not simply wild but literally untamed is this region in southwestern Utah; some of it remains unexplored even today. One mile beneath the earth's surface is a great bed of pure salt 3,000 feet thick. Three hundred million years ago, the sea, blocked in by upheavals of the land, evaporated, leaving the salt. Mud and sand accumulated and under heavy pressure hardened into today's rock. Only a small part of the canyonlands is encompassed by Canyonlands National Park. This picture was taken from the western sky early in the morning.

Moon over the Grand Canyon
Descending from Lake Powell through Marble Canyon, the Colorado River curves leftward between the wall at the upper right (Desert View) and Vishnu Temple. To the left of Vishnu Temple, which is in the center of the picture, is the mesa called Wotan's Throne. Climate in the canyon varies from desertic, at the bottom, to Arctic-Alpine. I took this photograph in mid March from Hopi Point, looking to the east. In the west and north, the walls were already in shadow, but in the east they shone in golden brightness under the rays of the setting sun.

Cliffs under the Evening Sun
This is the northern side of the Colorado River. The butte at the upper left is Zoroaster Temple; the large mesa below is Bradley Point. Jutting out like a peninsula at the right is Demaray Point (4,986 feet), which can be seen from the Yaki Point observation platform on the South Rim. We were flying about 2,300 feet lower than the elevation of Yaki Point, whose altitude is 7,259 feet. From this point, the Kaibab Trial goes north to the plateau of the same name. It was just before sunset, and the cliffs were a flamelike red.

The Grand Canyon in a Storm I
During the summer, I concentrated on taking pictures of thunderstorms. Every day, in the afternoon, thunder rolled, and thick, black clouds gathered on the North Rim. It was most dramatic when the entire canyon was enveloped in clouds. Then, as rain fell like a waterfall, the clouds turned gray. Kaibab Trail is to the upper right. In the upper center, the turretlike rock is Buddha Temple, below which is the dark mesa, Cheops Pyramid. Glowing darkly red to the left is Isis Temple. Captain Don Lopez de Cardenas discovered the canyon in 1540.

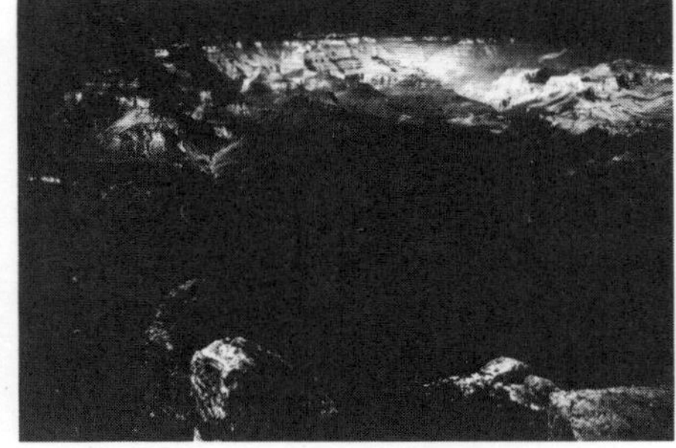

Chesler Park
This is the most dramatic scenery in Canyonlands National Park. From Monticello, Utah, we drove a jeep into the park and climbed Elephant Hill. It was like riding in an armored car with a very powerful engine. The fantasy world we saw from the top of Elephant Hill was the Needles, of which this is an aerial photograph. The wide space in the middle of the picture is called Chesler Park, and the butte in the center, Island. Evidence that the Anasazi (Ancient Ones) once lived in this area exists in the form of petroglyphs found in the canyons.

Green River Overlook
Twisting through the center of the picture is Green River, which joins the Colorado River in the central part of Canyonlands National Park, a little above Lake Powell. The two places offering a good view of the canyon are Green River Overlook and Grandview Point. In the early hours of a March morning, thirty minutes of camera work thoroughly numbed my fingers. In the upper left is Ekker Butte, and to the left of that is Elaterite Butte. To the right of the upper part of the withered tree is Turks Head. On the horizon are the Henry Mountains.

Old Faithful
The volcanic activity in this region has been going on for more than 40 million years. Mud volcanoes, hot springs, geysers and so on in the park number more than ten thousand. Old Faithful, the most famous of the geysers, blows once every 32 to 90 minutes to heights of as much as 180 feet. The duration is from 2 to 5 minutes. During our visit, it blew once for 4 minutes, but only to a height of a little more than 30 feet, apparently an unusual case. With its establishment on March 1, 1872, Yellowstone became the first national park in the world.

Rain Forest
Olympic National Park in the State of Washington has an area of 1,400 square miles lying in three sections, one mountainous, another heavily forested and the third a narrow strip of coastal cliffs and islands. Eight-thousand-foot-high Mount Olympus and its icefields are in the center. This photograph was taken as we were returning to the visitors' center on a forest trail. To the front and back, to the left and right, above and below, ferns and mosses carpeted the ground and hung from the trees, a beautiful green after the rain. It was like walking through a tunnel.

Geysers and Setting Sun
As the sun began to sink below the Rocky Mountains, the geyser at the left began to blow soundlessly. In the strong wind, it took only a few seconds for the vapor to be dispersed. I had read that geysers are most likely to blow in the evening, so after tramping through the swamps to approach them, I set up my equipment and waited. The number of geysers is quite large, but not all of them blow regularly. This picture was taken in Yellowstone National Park's Midway Geyser Basin, during the time we were camping at Madison Junction, Wyoming.

Minerva Terrace

Most of Yellowstone National Park lies in Wyoming, but there are narrow strips in Montana and Idaho. Near the northern entrance (in Montana) is Minerva Terrace, one of the Mammoth Hot Springs, so named because of their great volume of water. The temperature of the gurgling, hissing waters is above 98 degrees. Here minerals in the water have settled and crystalized, creating terraces in hues of yellow, green and purple. There are four other entrances, and the park is one of the greatest wildlife sanctuaries in the world.

Geysers of Firehole River

Returning from Old Faithful, I took this photograph of Midway Geyser Basin. Seen at the lower right, flowing from Shoshone Lake, is Firehole River; in the basin it passes through an evanescent host of geysers, which spew forth their hot vapors with a rumbling noise. The Continental Divide lies to the south and to the west. A series of earthquakes in August and September, 1959, made geysers more active and created at least one new one. Summer temperatures here range between 50 and 70 degrees but may fall below freezing even then.

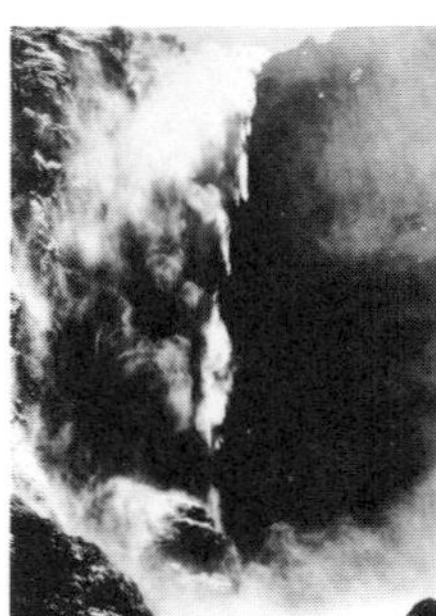

Bridalveil Fall

This is the most beautiful and delicate of Yosemite National Park's many waterfalls, but I am of the opinion that too many photographs of it have been taken. Although the best pictures are taken from the exit of Wawona Tunnel, we ventured into the spray to take this one at the foot of the falls with a wide-angle lens. In our search for the best light in which to photograph, we came here at the same time for several days. Ceded by the federal government to the State of California in 1864, Yosemite Valley and Mariposa Grove were the first state park.

black & white plates

Eroded Buttes

Seen here from Inspiration Point is Silent City in Bryce Canyon National Park. There is little snow on the steep buttes, and in this monochrome picture it is difficult to distinguish between the snow and the rock. Although it was April 1, it was like midwinter. We were surprised to awake in the morning and find three feet of snow on the roof of our car, and we had to walk through knee-deep snow to get to the observation platform. About one hundred years ago, the valley east of the park was settled by Mormons who were seeking religious freedom.

Wall of Windows

After walking one mile down a sloping path from Bryce Point, we came to Loop Trail and took this picture. This wall of rock, which stands between Bryce Point and Inspiration Point, is evidence of the elevation during the last 13 million years of the floors of ancient lakes and seas, after which wind and water shaped the limestone and sandstone. After making several visits here, I found that, rather than a fine day, the best photographs could be taken when dark clouds cast shadows. Not long after taking this picture, we were drenched by a thundershower.

Spider Rock

The innermost of the five observation platforms in Canyon de Chelly National Monument is at Spider Rock. The road leading there changes from paved to gravel, and when I was there in April, the snow was thawing, the mud was three feet deep, and the jeep literally waddled. This photograph, however, was taken in the summer; conditions were much better than in April when half of the scenery was snow covered. Spider Rock is in the center. In the upper center are the upper reaches of Canyon de Chelly, and to the right, Monument Canyon.

Broken Layers of Sandstone
A living specimen of the might of moving water, these rocks were formed 200 million years ago during the Permian period of the late Paleozoic era. What formed the rock was pressure; its shape is due to erosion. The magnificent wall of broken sandstone in this picture, taken from the White House observation platform in Canyon de Chelly, is to the left of the Indian ruins. In Canyon del Muerto is a cave called Massacre Cave, where the Spanish killed more than one hundred Navajos during a day-long battle in 1805.

Bird's-eye View of the Grand Canyon II
In this early morning photograph taken from near Little Colorado, the sharp butte in the upper left is Vishnu Temple. The round butte in the lower left is Rama Shrine, and Wotan's Throne is the long white plateau at the upper right. A little lower, the triangular mountain is Freya Castle. Mountains in the foreground are unnamed. This is the eastern part of the canyon. In the upper right part of the picture is the Colorado River. Viewed from the air, it can be seen that the walls of the canyon consist of hills and valleys, not one layer of rock.

Before the Storm I
A sudden wind came in the wake of thunder rolling from the North Rim of the Grand Canyon as we were taking photographs from Hopi Point on the South Rim. Millions of years ago before the canyon was formed, the Colorado River was a slow-moving stream wandering through the plateau. In the upper center of the picture, looking like an owl in flight, is Vishnu Temple. Wotan's Throne is to the left of that and lower; to the left is Cape Royal. On the right in deep shadow is O'Neil Butte; below that is the base of Yavapai Point.

The Grand Canyon in a Storm II
Because of the great width of the canyon (four to eighteen miles), it is rare for thunderclouds to cover the whole canyon at one time. The clouds before the storm build to great heights. We were taking photographs from Hopi Point, and when the rain began to fall there, the sky beyond the North Rim began to clear. Appearing as two small hills in the center of the picture are Osiris Temple, to the left, and Claude Birdseye Point, to the right. Below them is the Tower of Set. At the extreme right is Cheops Pyramid, below which is Dana Butte.

Salt Creek II
Our visits to Canyonlands National Park were made in March, July and October. This photograph of Salt Creek Drainage was taken from the air on an evening in October. During the spring, the air was so turbulent that photography was nearly impossible. Conditions in summer were little more favorable. In the fall, we stayed here one week, the weather was beautiful, and we were able to take pictures in the morning, afternoon and evening. The altitude in the park ranges from 3,600 to nearly 7,000 feet above sea level.

Before the Storm II
The Grand Canyon, standing in what was once a comparatively flat plateau, has a length of 218 miles. Lake Mead is southwest of Lake Powell, but between the two, stretches of the river flow in every direction. All storm pictures were taken in early August, the storms often appearing at places I wanted to photograph. I found it difficult to take pictures that met my expectations. Brahma Temple is in the center. To the right is Zoroaster Temple, and the rather dark spot to the left is Deva Temple. This was taken from Hopi Point on the South Rim.

Sequoia Struck by Lightning
In the Giant Forest in Sequoia National Park, California, is Circle Meadow. In the Sierra Nevada, thunderclouds form almost every summer day. It was a terrible sight to see trees two and three hundred feet high that had been split asunder by thunderbolts. This tree, where it had been split, had carbonized, but at the top of the tree new branches were growing, indicating that it was still alive. Sequoia and neighboring Kings Canyon National parks exist primarily for the preservation of the giant trees, but Mount Whitney is also here.

Sequoia Roots

This tree must have fallen many years ago, for the large, dense roots, measuring about twenty-five feet, had begun to rot. Still, they presented a magnificent sight. This picture was taken north of Sequoia's Giant Forest, in the woods above Generals' Highway. The trunk of the tree lying across the roots was also a good subject for photography. I used a super wide-angle lens and because it was very dark, strobe light. The trees, whether standing or lying, are not only big but old and once grew in Europe and Asia as well. One species still grows in China.

Tallest Tree on Earth

It is estimated that 3,000 to 3,500 years have passed since this tree was a sapling, making it the oldest tree alive. It is named after General Sherman; many of the trees in Sequoia and Kings Canyon National parks are named after Civil War generals and men who have been president of the United States. It stands 272.4 feet high, and its diameter and circumference at the base are 36.5 and 114.6 feet respectively. The trunk alone weighs 625 tons, and the whole tree, more than twice that. To take this picture from behind the tree, I used a super wide-angle lens.

View from Washburn Point

The topography and climate in California are both extremely varied. Because Yosemite Valley is only 1,970 feet above sea level and the Sierra Nevada rises to heights of more than 14,000 feet, the best view of the park can be obtained from a high point. Washburn Point (7,370 feet) is the highest observation platform in the Sierra Nevada. This photograph was taken in the afternoon in an easterly direction. The higher fall, to the right, is Nevada (594 feet), and the one in the center is Vernal (317 feet). This place is near the famous Glacier Point.

Yosemite Falls

This waterfall, dropping 2,425 feet, is not only the highest in Yosemite National Park but the most famous. I took this photograph at the beginning of June, when water was still plentiful; in summer, the water thins to a trickle, and in August usually disappears. It was taken from a chapel in Yosemite Village at midday. Later in the afternoon, the lower fall was in shadow, but it was evening before darkness came to the upper fall. Wind caught the water as it fell, so I found it difficult to compose this picture. The floor of the valley is small.

EARTH'S DIURNAL COURSE

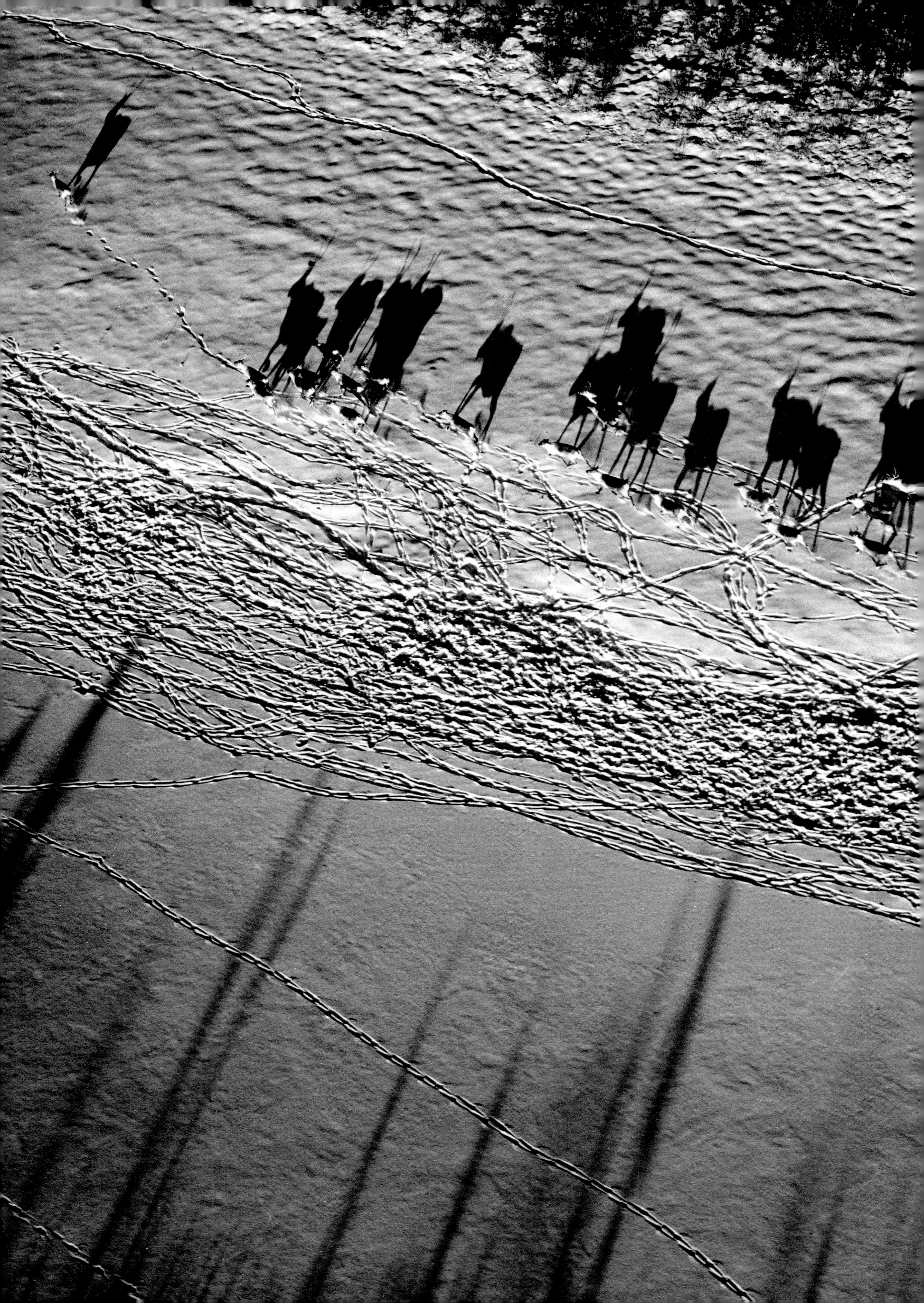

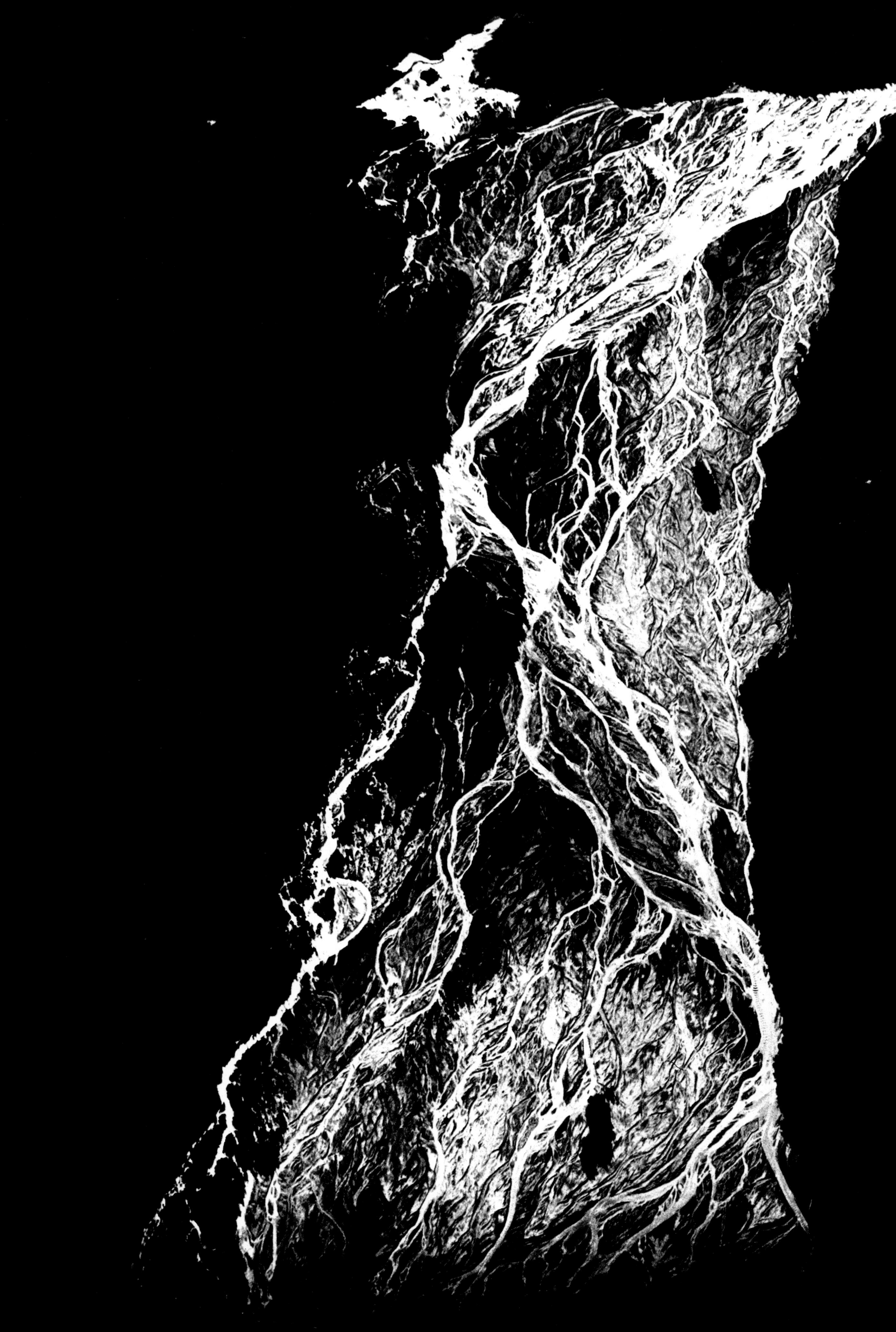

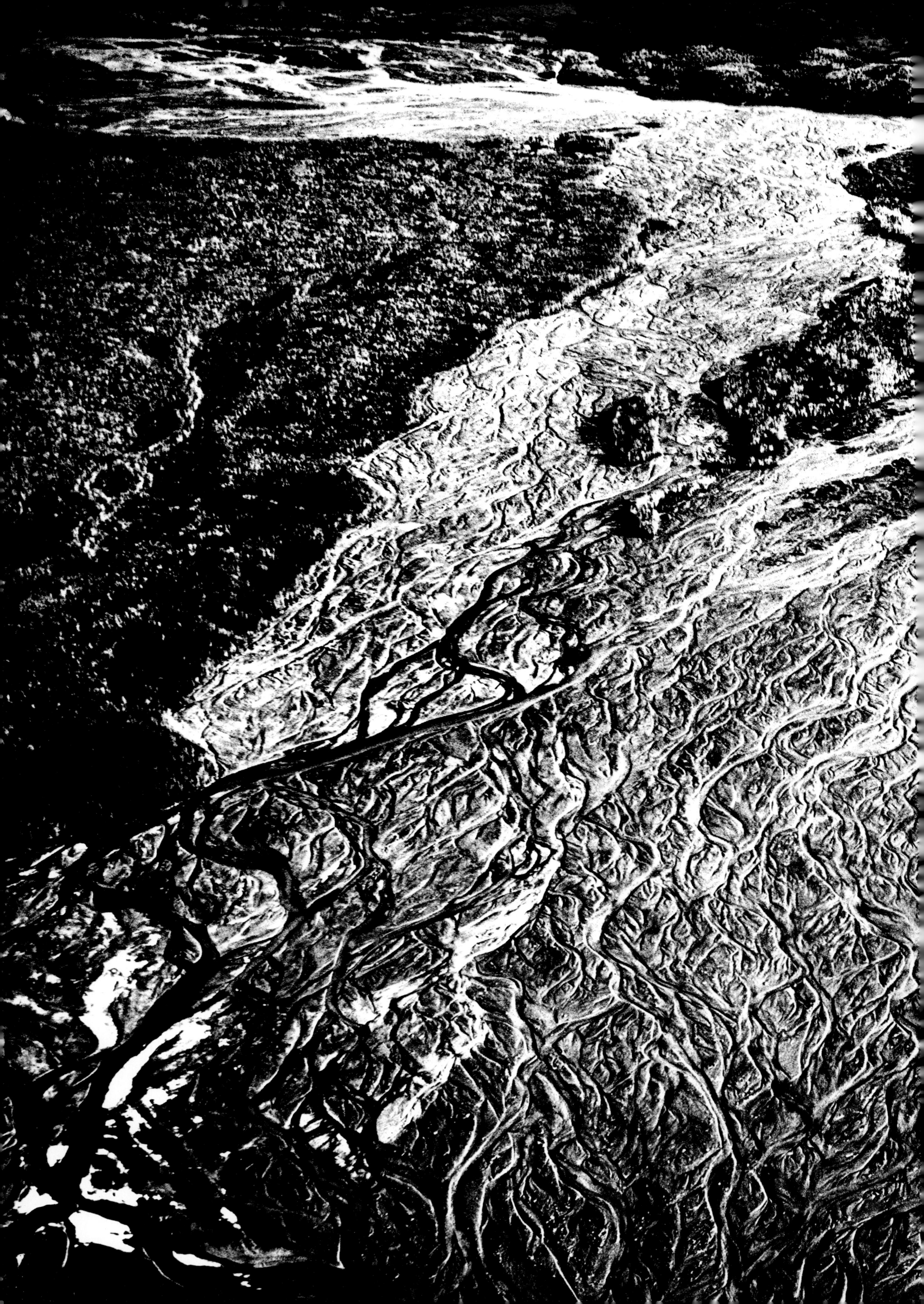

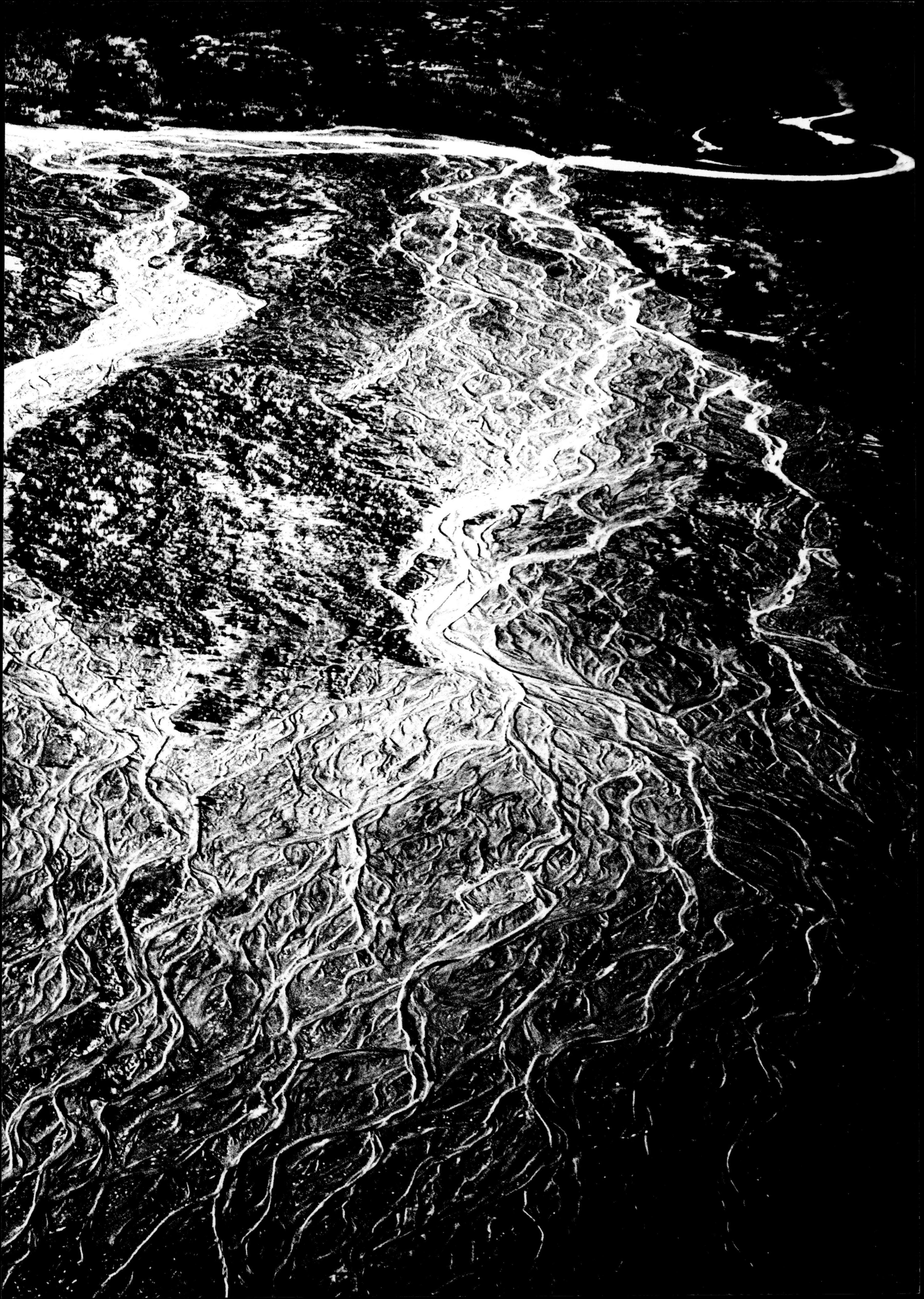

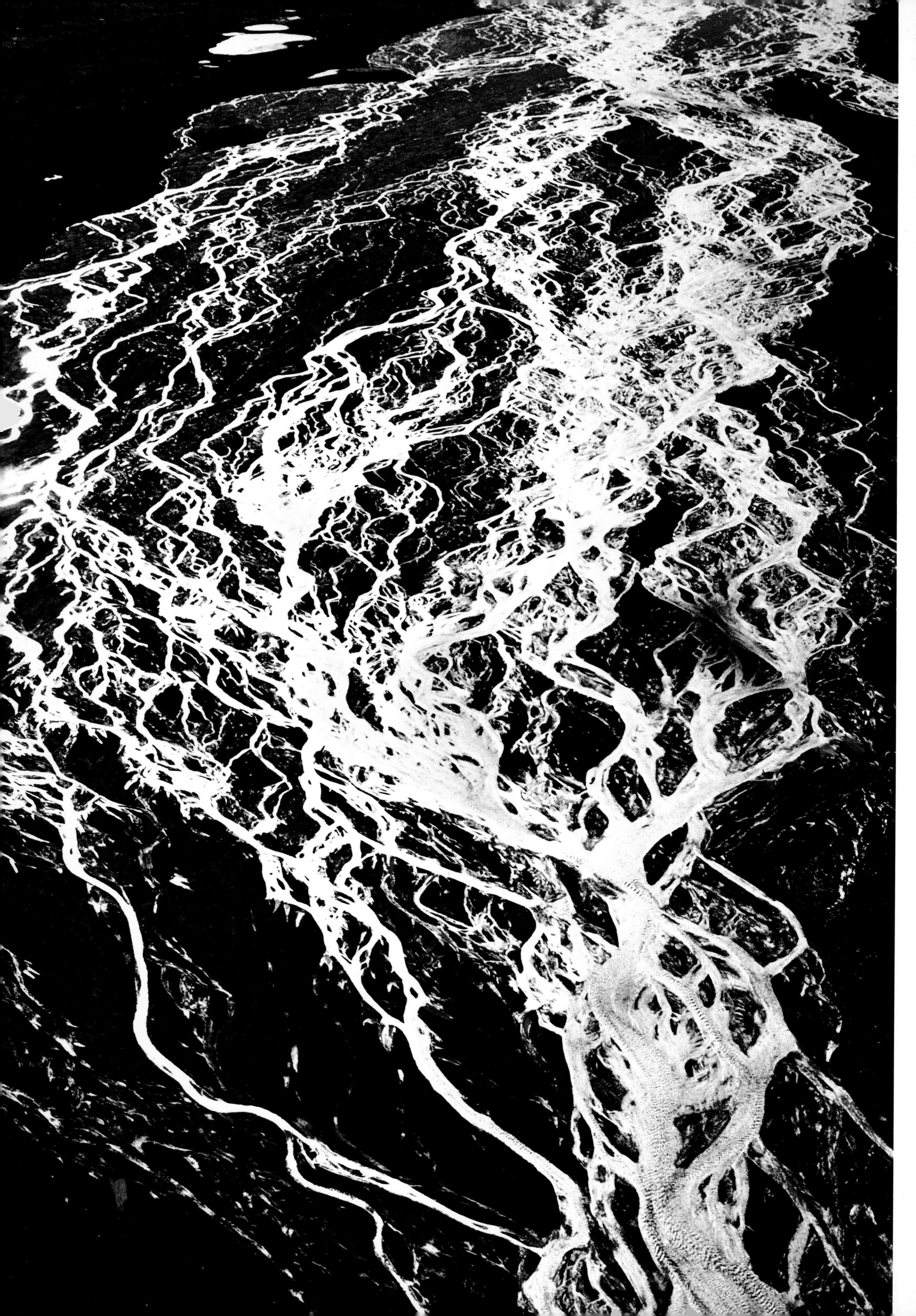

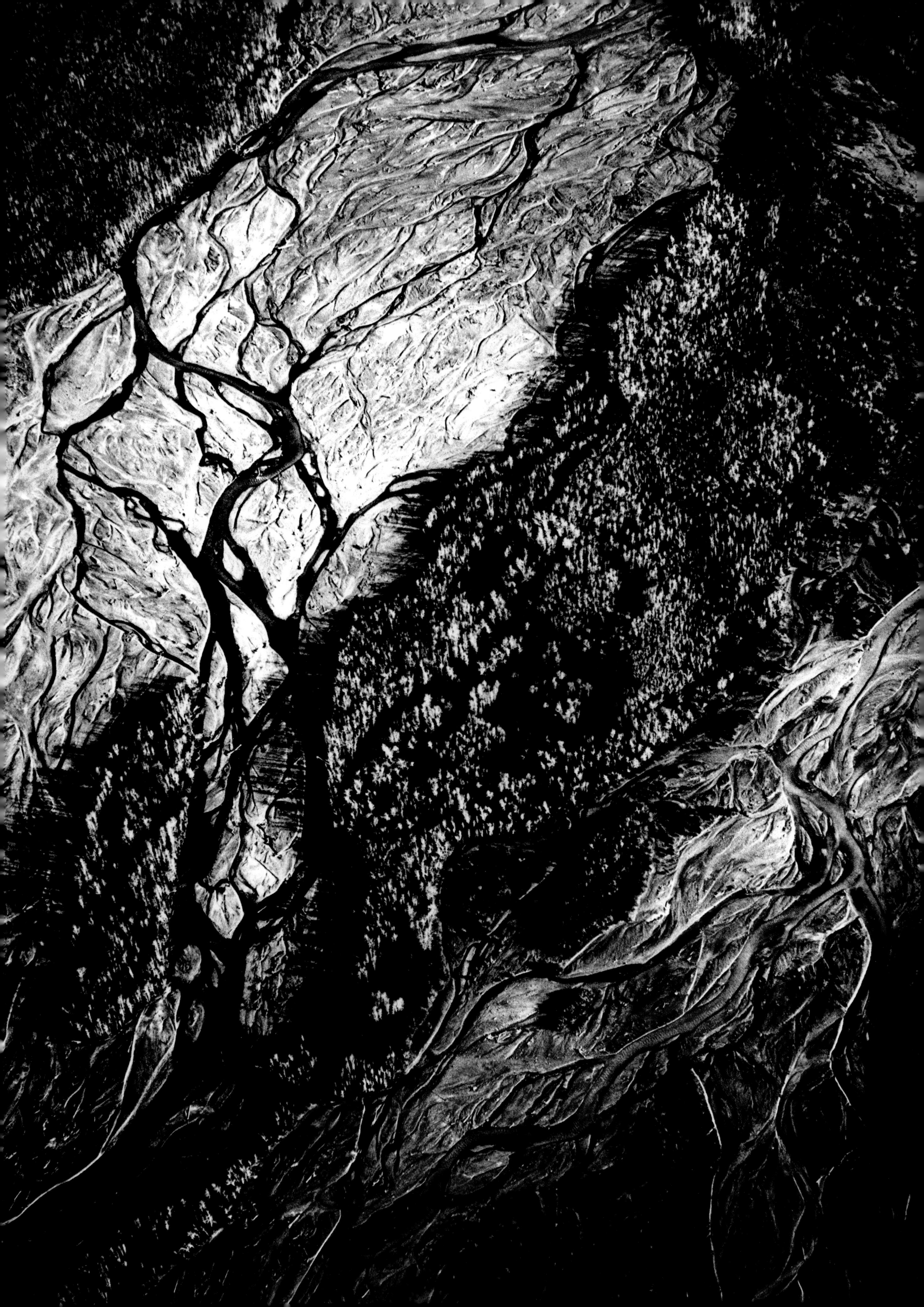

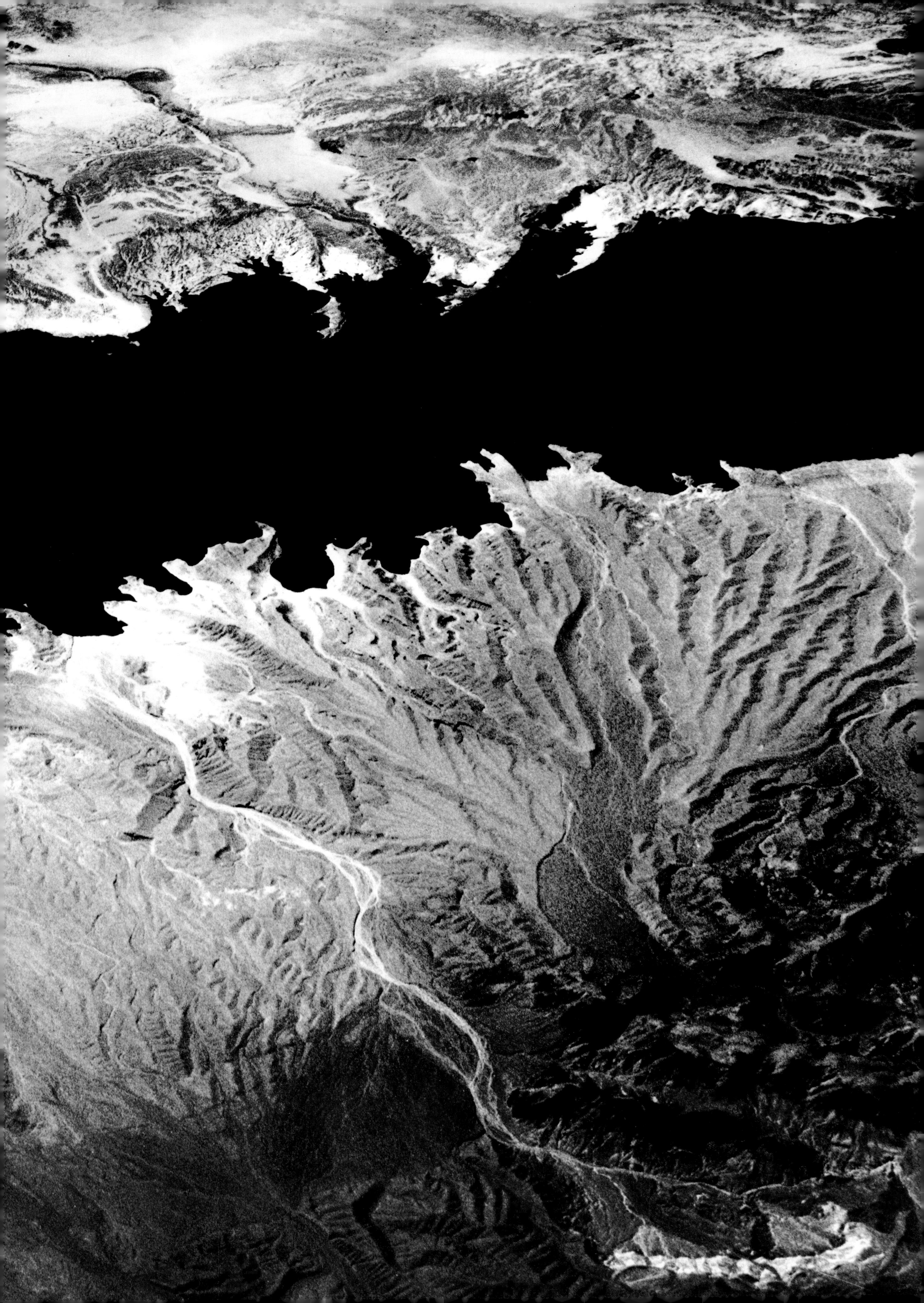

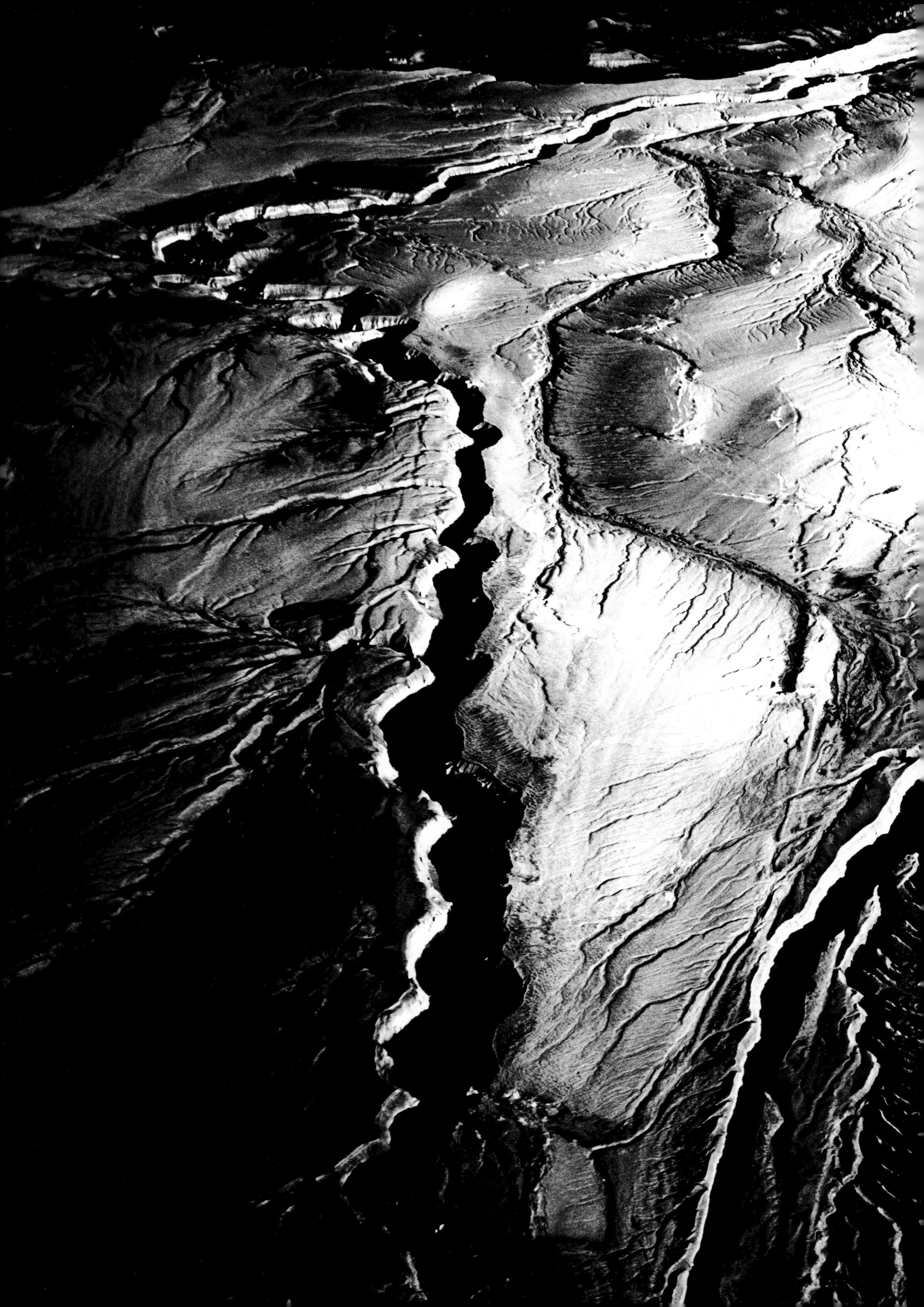

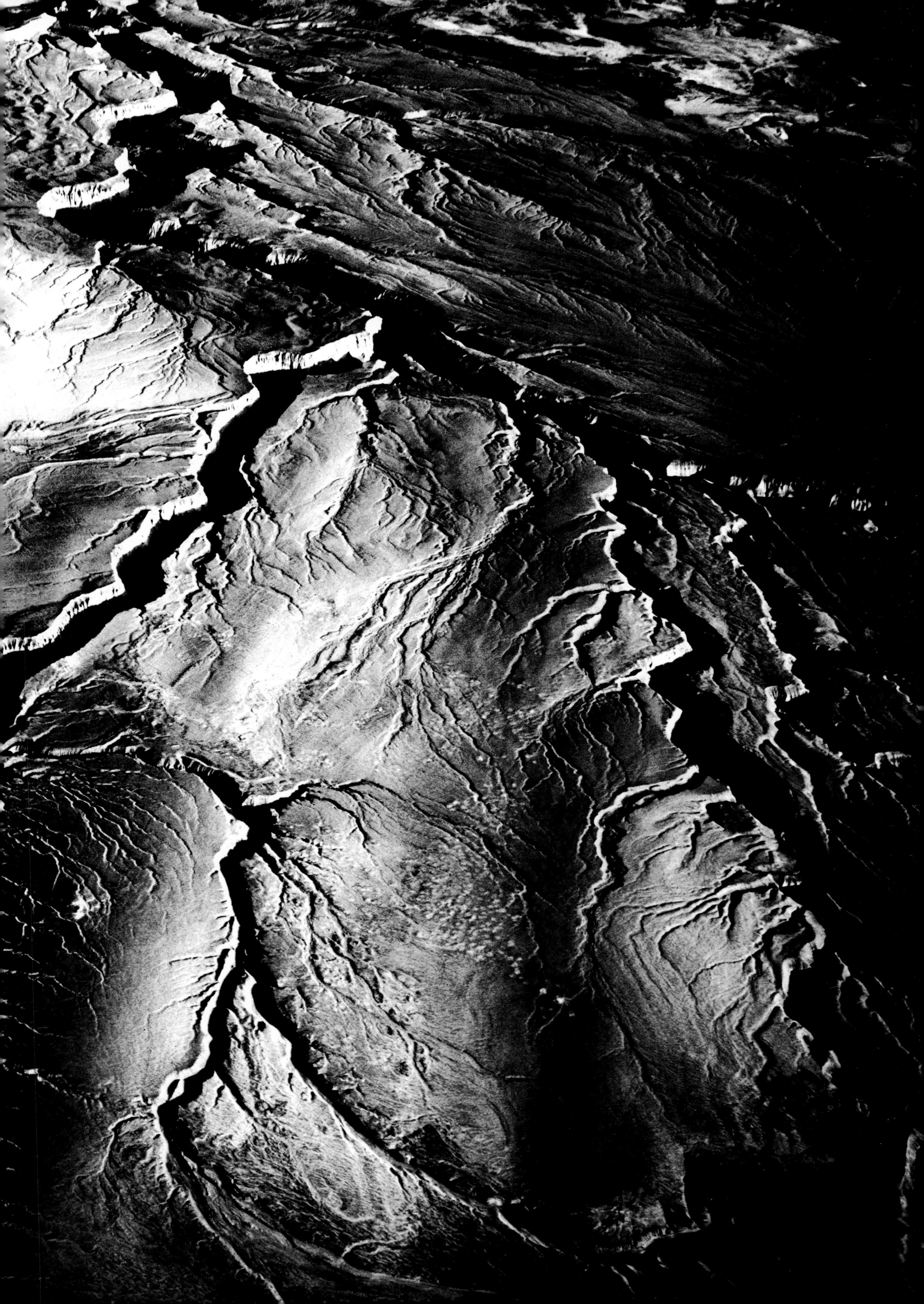

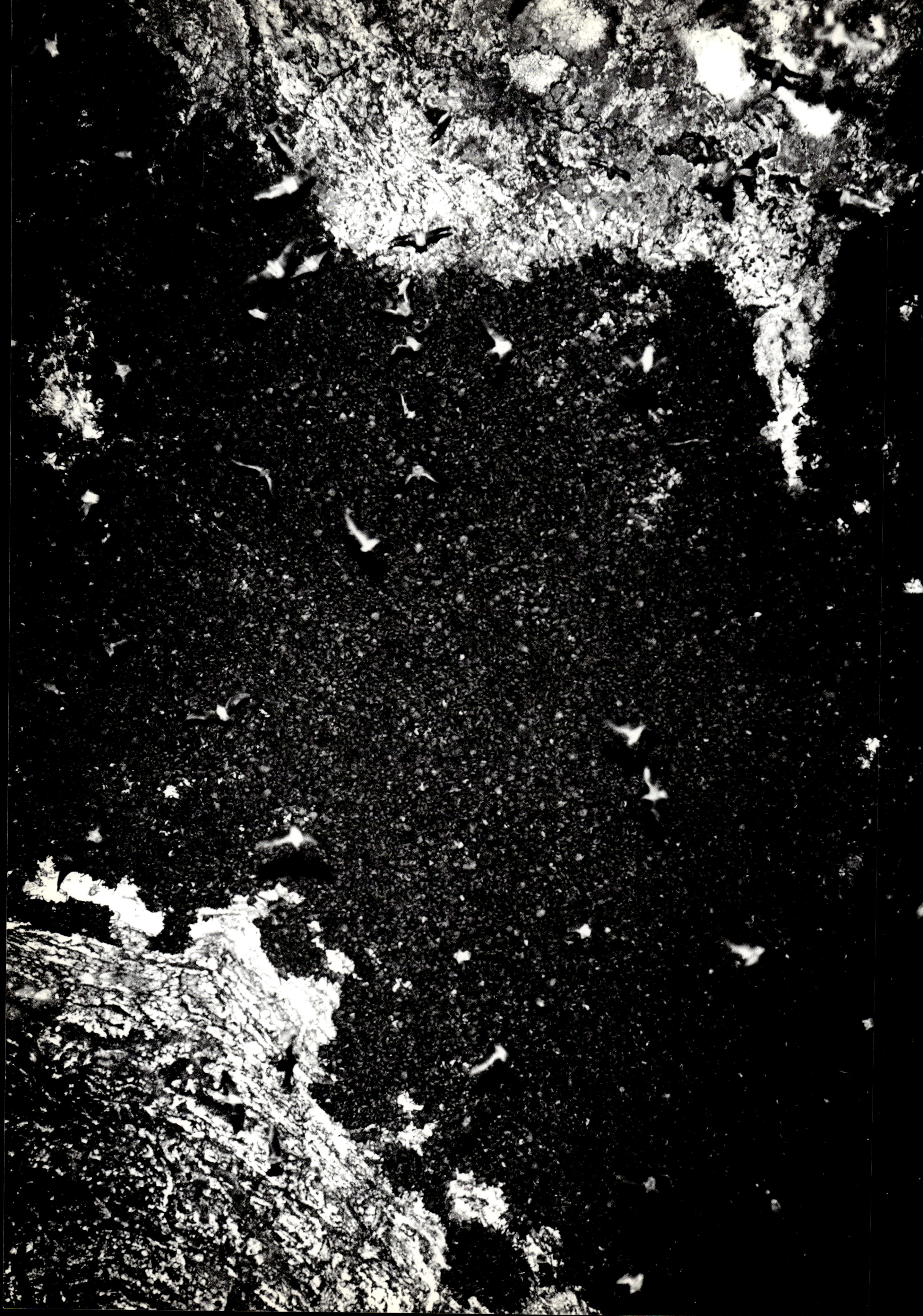

Earth's Diurnal Course

A decade before my photographic journey to the United States, while on my way from Europe to South America, I had passed the time waiting for my plane in New York by browsing through aviation magazines. In one I came across a picture that, despite its amateurish quality, impressed me. It depicted a colossal herd of animals, which I took to be reindeer, crossing a snowy plain. From the caption, I jotted down "Brooks Range" in my notebook.

I went through many notebooks, but the image of that great herd remained with me for several years. When the time came for me to chart a course for the photography for this book, I decided that I would not include pictures of human beings, nor would I include pictures of man-made objects such as buildings, roads and so on. My lens would be aimed primarily at the earth itself, but still I reached the conclusion that my mission would not be accomplished until I myself took pictures of those great animals, which, I learned, were caribou, or reindeer under another name.

In Alaska, I had the opportunity (if it can be called that) of seeing a freshly shot caribou corpse. I must admit that it was much larger than I had imagined, being four or five times larger than the tame deer that freely roam the parks in the ancient Japanese capital of Nara. And the antlers were enormous. It was interesting to learn that this is the only species of deer in which both the buck and the doe have antlers (shed annually, in midwinter by the buck and in the spring by the doe).

Now that there was no doubt about the animal's existence, I had only to locate that large herd that I wanted to photograph in its natural habitat. Before my departure, a letter from America informed me that there was no need to go to the Brooks Range; Mount McKinley was on my schedule, and I would be able to see the caribou at the same time that I was taking pictures of the mountains and glaciers. But I found not a single one, though we searched every day.

At the home of Don Sheldon, our pilot, one of his friends listened to my story and advised me that the caribou in the Wrangell Mountains, two hundred miles to the east of Talkeetna, were much finer than those in the environs of McKinley. According to him they were fatter and the meat was more palatable. This, I must confess, was the first time that I had heard that caribou were shot for food.

The McKinley Range was unable to yield the object of my search, I was unable to go to the Wrangells at that time, and it was several months before I went, after all, to the Brooks Range. From California, we flew to Alaska for the third time, changing planes at Anchorage and Fairbanks and arriving in the village of Bettles Field, a little north of the Arctic Circle, on November 2. In Anchorage, winter was beginning; in the Arctic it had set in, everything frozen.

The following day, after pumping hot air through a duct into the plane engine to warm it up, we started off. There were only about six hours between sunrise and sunset, and Shanahan, our pilot, thought our search would be difficult, because the number of caribou has decreased drastically in recent years. Relying on Shanahan's knowledge of their habits and his intuition, we flew first over the frozen lakes where caribou are likely to gather during the daytime. After two hours of flying, nothing. About to give up, we had changed course and crossed a large mountain, when Shanahan raised his voice above the noise of the engine and said, "Look! There they are."

Far below, there were some small animals. We descended and I opened the window and focused my camera. "They" were exactly six caribou, not the large herd I had had my heart set on. We circled several times and I was able to take some pictures; nevertheless, I was disappointed. We climbed again and spotted some small black dots on the lakes, which were caribou. During my stay, the largest herd we found numbered only about fifty.

It was only a few years ago that herds numbered in the thousands. Hunters have been responsible for bringing them near to extinction, for the district is not forbidden to men with guns. Their herd instinct makes it easier for the hunters, as does the caribou's lack of fear of man. If a plane lands, rather than run away, they will approach, even running toward the muzzles of waiting guns. Their behavior contrasts with that of moose, which run away, take cover under trees, and remain immobile. Because of this, though we spotted some moose, I could not get any good pictures.

Though caribou are fast swimmers and also have a swinging trot and the stamina to keep it up mile after mile, an airplane is much faster. When overtaken on the tundra, they will stand stock-still. We once circled over a female and her two calves; they had no place to escape to. Their tales pointed at our plane. It is hard to believe, but hunters pursue them in this fashion and direct their fire from the window of the plane. This is clearly a violation of the spirit of hunting. Caribou are not the only endangered species, but they are an example.

Alaska—with the great variation in the length of its day, its glaciers, its volcanoes, and water, water everywhere—is remindful of the extremes and changes that the earth, the universe knows so well and indicative of the fact that the world is not all terra firma. But the place I chose to view fossils was the Petrified Forest in Arizona. Here too, we came across vandalism.

March was the month of our first visit, despite information I had received that winter weather was bad, with lots of rain and snow. It seemed reasonable to assume that snow would not last long in the desert.

The park was on a much smaller scale than many we visited, being only sixteen miles long from north to south. For visitors, there are yard-wide, paved paths. Straying from the regular path through knee-deep mud left by the last big rain, I sought out the objects that would make the best picture. My search for fossils of good shape and color lasted three days on that occasion.

Where had all the fossils gone? The formation of the petrified wood here and in other places in the Southwest began a long time ago, some 150 to 185 million years before recorded history, with conifer forests first being covered with volcanic ash brought by floods. A lack of oxygen kept the trees from rotting, while water containing silica seeped into the fibers. Over time, the silica turned into quartz, a mineral as common as common can be, but in this case cryptocrystalline quartz, similar to jade or agate. The ash was still there, but at some time the crust of the earth rose, and in some places the forest of long ago was exposed.

Despite dire warnings that persons who disturb the petrified remains will be punished under the laws of the State of Arizona—printed in, among other places, the guidebook—there are tacked on the walls of the visitors' center at Rainbow Forest a great number of letters of apology. These are written and signed by those who got caught. Pockets are a convenient place into which to slip small pieces; altogether, it is estimated that twelve tons of fossils are carried off each year, bit by bit, piece by piece. I saw only large fossil remains, many chipped smooth.

It was dryer when I went the second time, in the middle of July. Besides daytime pictures, I wanted to photograph the trees of long ago before dawn came, red sky in the east. Here was nature's mysterious drama unfolded over scores of millions of years. Fortunately, the park superintendent lent us the key to the park, and we could leave our motel at three in the morning and be inside the gate by four. It is, however, very difficult to fix on film the image of the mind's eye.

The Colorado River has done more than create the spectacle of the Grand Canyon. From the western slopes of the Rocky Mountains, it passes through the states of Colorado, Utah, Arizona, forms the Arizona-Nevada and Arizona-California borders, and juts forty miles into Mexico before angling into the Gulf of California. Although it is only the eleventh longest river in North America, it is a mighty river, nearly fifteen hundred miles long, cutting slowly but deeply into the earth and forming canyons and lakes of incredible grandeur. One of its great tributaries is the Green River, but there are others—the San Juan, the Little Colorado, the Gila, the Gunnison, the Dolores, the Virgin. It would take a whole book of photographs to capture all its attendant grandness. My intention, however, was not to classify my photographs geographically, but according to nature—more than that: nature at its finest.

The wildest of the wild places I saw with my own eyes (outside Alaska) was Canyonlands National Park in Utah, which I visited three times. The roads, in the north and east of the park, are few and unpaved. During my first trip at the end of March, I went to the northern part, to Island in the Sky, where there are two observation platforms, Grandview Point and Green River Overlook. Deep snow kept me from Grandview Point, so I could only take pictures from the latter. It was cold, and in the early morning, finger-numbing cold.

On my second visit in July, I was able to use my camera from the 6,034-foot Grandview Point. There was the desertic land, cleft by the Colorado and Green rivers and stretching out forty miles before the eye. The gorges and buttes seemed to me like the entrance to hell. One thousand feet below was White Rim; one thousand feet below that flowed the Colorado.

The road leading to the eastern entrance of the park branches off the road connecting Moab and Monticello. The pavement stops at the entrance. There we transferred to a jeep and climbed Elephant Hill. Breathtaking indeed was the view of the Needles, a seemingly uncountable number of rocky spires soaring into the sky and being reflected in pools of water at their feet.

The air of spring and summer was turbulent, so much so that I was barely able to remain seated in the plane, to say nothing of taking a good picture. But in October, I was able to do aerial photography, so I concentrated on that. In Canyonlands, there are places, like the Maze, that no human being is known to have entered, and there are also curves in the Colorado that can be photographed only from the air. In one portion of the upper reaches of the river, it is joined by tributaries and forms a sprawling figure eight. This place is called the Loop and is one of nature's most extraordinary creations.

It was astonishing to see the result of using infrared film from a jet plane traveling thirty-two thousand feet above the earth. The course and junction of the Green and Colorado are shown just as they are on a map and with complete accuracy. Moreover, all that is beyond the capability of the human eye or ordinary film became visible with ease.

I also saw nature underground. It was the first time that I had ever seen a stalactite cavern on such a huge scale. This was Carlsbad Caverns in New Mexico.

On my first visit, it was the end of February and very snowy, but the park was crowded and photography was impossible, until I was able to obtain permission to go, accompanied by rangers, into the caves before and after visiting hours. Because there are more than fifty caves, a round of them takes some time, and because of the darkness I used strobe light, taking two pictures simultaneously with two cameras having lenses of different focal lengths.

The Big Room is called that because of its size. It is nearly three hundred feet high, and its perimeter measures about one and one-quarter miles. There is a stalactite, called Giant Dome, in front of the entrance that has a diameter of ten feet. Inside is a long, thin pillar known as the Totem Pole, quite unlike the rocky "totem poles" I had seen in Monument Valley.

Another cavern that impressed me deeply was the Kings Palace, where nature has extravagantly created perfect works of art. Hanging from the ceiling were stalactites as thin as a piece of paper, long ones like so many sticks of molten candy, and tens of thousands of others beyond description. Man, with only his hands, could not, I thought, create such beautiful forms; I found it hard to believe that in this world such a beautiful place still existed.

Being 250 million years old, the caves were as old or older than any of the other wonders of nature I had seen. Here deep inside the Guadalupe Mountains was an embodiment of the action of water on stone.

We made our second trip, to see bats, in the middle of September. The bats have inhabited the caves for thousands of years, though not permanently. Migrating northward from Mexico in the summer, as many as three million may congregate in one cave. But their number is believed to have diminished by one million, because of the use of agricultural chemicals, which kill insects, which are food for bats—man unbalancing nature.

The bats leave the caves at night. Before this happened, we could hear the screeching of about ten sentinels, apparently giving an all-clear signal. Then vast waves of flying mammals pour from the mouths of the cave, creating a feeling of fear and horror.

To protect spectators from the viruses carried by these furry creatures, highly elevated bleachers have been built, over which they do not fly. To photograph the animals in the caves, we risked that danger, first putting on gas masks, then being guided by the park rangers. Using strong strobe flash, we took pictures for five evenings.

The odor of the bat guano is extremely unpleasant and penetrated even our gas masks. Wanting to take pictures of sleeping bats, we entered a cave one afternoon and found the floor covered with guano to a depth of three feet. It got into our shoes and onto our hands. The smell was overpowering. We could hardly breathe. Never before in my life had returning to the great out-of-doors been more refreshing.

Hundreds of thousands of tons of the guano have been carried away to be used as fertilizer, but the floor was still thick with it. Although we put up with these conditions for more than an hour, we found not a single bat, for they had fled into an inner cave. This may have been due to their having been frightened by the flashes we used on previous evenings. The rangers took us into the inner cavern and flashed their lights on the ceiling. There they were, indeed, great hordes of them hanging down, all but completely hiding the rock. And again, we saw sentinel bats, sending out warnings of approaching danger. The darkness made it difficult for me to focus my camera, but I finally took pictures with a 300-mm telephoto lens at settings from 100 to 160 feet in increments of 15 feet, discovering thereby that the height of the cave was 160 feet.

The caves, with their stalactites, their stalagmites, their bats, were a thrilling experience for us and a statement that the wonders of nature can be seen even beneath the earth's surface.

Earth's Diurnal Course

color plates

Caribou I

Once I saw a picture of a large herd of these huge animals, and I knew that they are native to Canada and Alaska. My expectations when I traveled to the Brooks Range were great. Although my search lasted an entire week, it ended in disappointment. The great herds have been nearly annihilated by merciless hunters, who seem to regard the tundra as a happy hunting ground. This photograph of a small herd of caribou fleeing from an ice-covered lake into the forest was taken in the middle of an intensely cold arctic November.

Tundra

Anywhere one goes in Alaska, he will find a great number of swamps and lakes, particularly the latter. When I took this early morning picture at the beginning of May, the ice on the lakes was still thick. The dark spots are forests of mostly deciduous trees. We were near the small village of Talkeetna and looking in a westerly direction. Floating down the Susitna River were huge chunks of ice, the only indication that spring was near, for I could see no buds on the trees. The river, several miles wide, skirts the edge of Mount McKinley National Park.

Petrified Forest

Between Flagstaff and Gallup, Arizona, is the small (147-square-mile) Petrified Forest National Park. Once upon a time, trees, resembling pine, were covered by mud and sand, and since oxygen was scarce, they did not decay. The water that seeped into them contained silica, and the silica crystalized into quartz. The rich colors are due to oxides of manganese and iron. I took this photograph in the Long Logs section of Rainbow Forest in the middle of summer. During the spring thaw, searching for the trees involved wading through knee-deep mud.

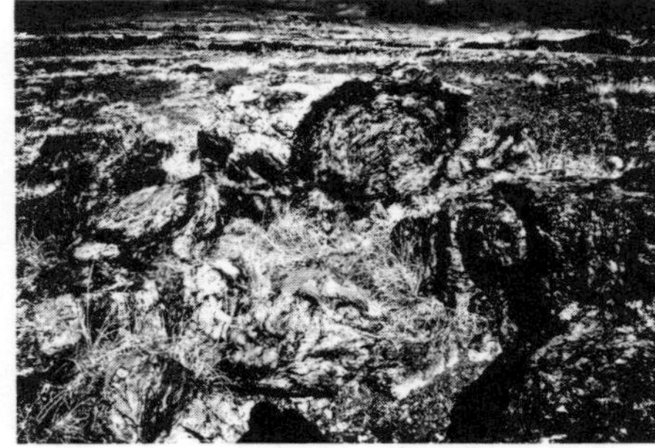

Fossils and the Sun

"Anyone who steals fossils, no matter how small they may be, will be subject to a fine or imprisonment or both under state law." To enforce this stricture, which is quoted in the guidebook to the Petrified Forest, triple-barred gates are closed at night, but by special permission, we were able to enter the park by 4 A.M. every day. Using flash, we took photographs of the plant fossils. I wanted to capture the mystery of nature expressed in the drama of their creation. Prior to a great uplifting of the earth, the region was under 3,000 feet of soil.

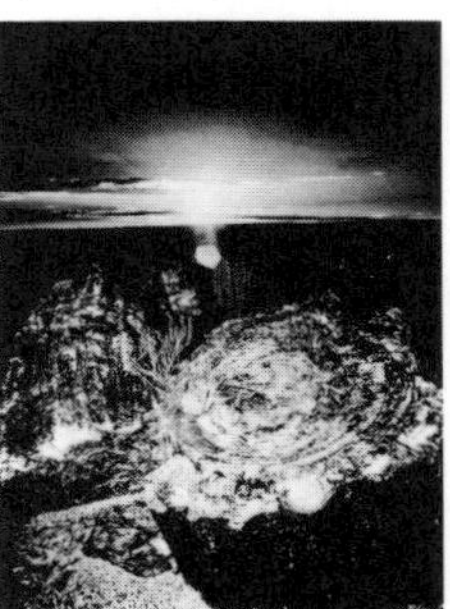

black & white plates

Caribou II

My search for caribou began in 1971 and was continued in 1973; on both occasions I began, by car and by plane, near Mount McKinley, where it has been confirmed that large herds existed some years ago. It was in vain, and the only animals I found were mountain goats and bear. Predators range from the parasitic botfly to human beings. The animals themselves—herds once numbered in the thousands—do damage the fragile tundra. I went north to the Arctic Circle looking for the elusive beasts, but, sad to say, I found only a few.

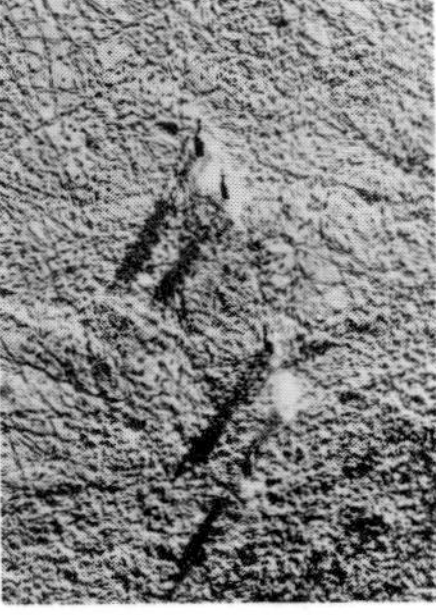

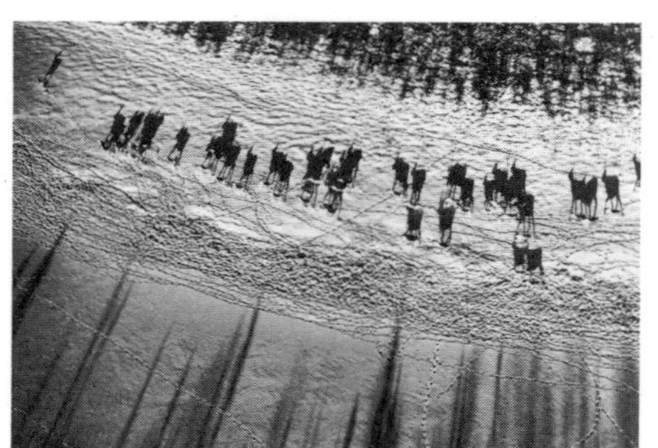

Caribou III

Four or five years ago, it is said, when one landed on a frozen lake, the caribou, perhaps out of curiosity, would come to greet one. Seeing a hunter aim a rifle, they would run—toward the hunter. I was also told that hunters shot these large members of the deer family from low-flying planes. In this precarious environment, the animals were for the Eskimo not only food but material for clothing, tools and many other things. In the latter part of the nineteenth century, the herds became so depleted that reindeer were imported from northern Europe.

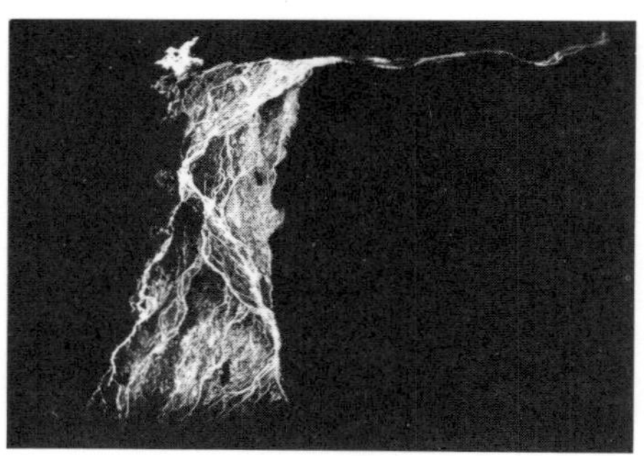

Foraker River

From Mount McKinley's Straightway Glacier flows a river, and from Foraker Glacier on the mountain of the same name flows another river. They meet at the foot of the mountains, northwest of Mount McKinley. To take the best picture possible, we circled over this area more than a dozen times. The best result was the one taken from this angle, about five miles downriver from the junction. The dark spots are forests. Although the climb is hazardous, the challenge of Mount McKinley lies not so much in its height as in its remote location.

Rainbow River I

This photograph is of the upper reaches of the river, into which pour melting snow and glacial ice. In the middle of Katmai National Monument, two mountains (Mount Snowy, 7,090 feet, and Mount Denison, 7,605 feet) are connected by Serpent Tongue Glacier, from which more than a dozen smaller glaciers branch off into the valleys. One wonders at the terrible floods that would result if there were a sudden rise in temperature. From the air, the river's tributaries look like thin streams. The park extends halfway across the Alaska Peninsula.

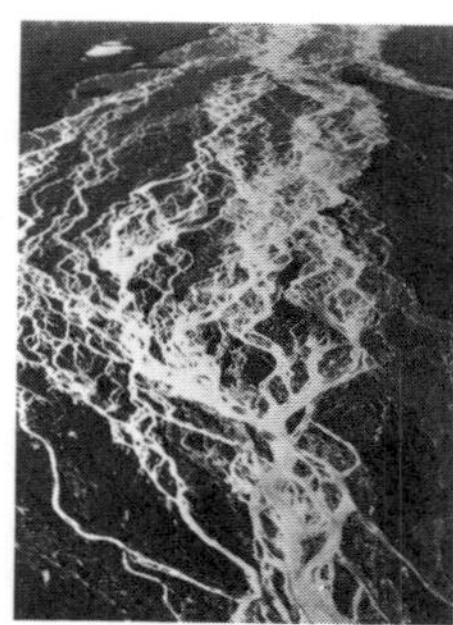

McKinley River

Originating from Muldrow Glacier, this is one of scores of streams that flow into the Yukon River, which wanders across central Alaska, then turns south and west again on its way to the Bering Sea, about 2,000 miles altogether. After our search for caribou ended in failure, we flew to the north side of the McKinley range to see this river spreading its pattern across the plain. I took more than a dozen pictures but could not find the proper balance between the pattern and the sun shining on the waters. This picture was taken in a westerly direction.

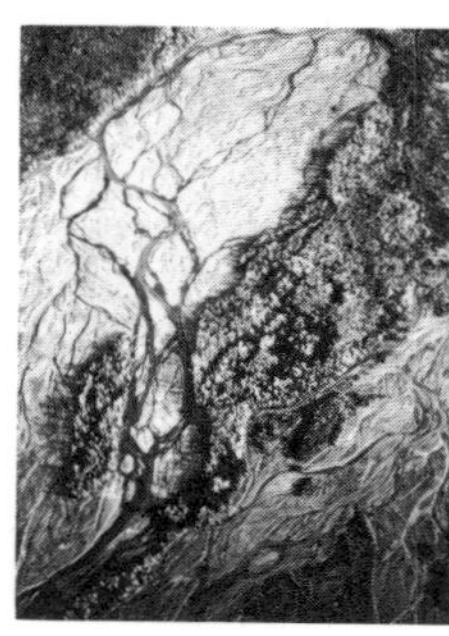

Rainbow River II

This is a muddy tributary of Rainbow River, taken at a place where the river flooded and tore up a forest after the thaw. Katmai National Monument is isolated from civilization, and all visitors come by plane or boat, for there are no automobile roads. Here, more than in any other national park in the country, exist vestiges of nature in its primordial state. With an area of 4,362 square miles, it is the second largest national park and is about three-fifths the size of Shikoku, the smallest of the four main Japanese islands.

The Maze

We were flying in a jet plane at an altitude of slightly more than six miles when I took this photograph of the southern half of Canyonlands National Park. In the center is a group of canyons, which no human has ever entered, known as The Maze. In the upper right is Green River. The point where it joins the Colorado River is at the right center. Downstream from that point is Lake Powell. The hollow in the center is Spanish Bottom, to the left of which is the famous Cataract Canyon. At the lower right are the Needles.

Lake Mead

In the upper left of this photograph of Lake Mead are the Muddy Mountains and the promontory called Blue Point. At the left is Echo Bay. The Valley of Fire is in the upper right. To the left of the long, white peninsula is Calico Bay, and to its right is Rogers Bay. To the right of the latter is Fire Bay. Further to the right are Black Point and then Salt Bay and Salt Point. At the lower right of the picture flows Lime Wash. Hoover Dam holds back the lake. This picture was taken from a plane flying at an altitude of 32,000 feet.

Mouth of the Colorado River

By the time it crosses the Mexican border and enters the Bay of California, the Colorado River has traveled nearly fifteen hundred miles, about twice the air distance from Colorado Springs, near which it rises. Great volumes of earth are carried to the delta, which used to be sixty miles further inland, but the construction of dams has reduced the amount, and the delta is no longer the huge swampland it once was. At its peak, the flow of water into the gulf, seen in the upper part of the picture, is measured in thousands of tons per second.

Bird's-eye View of Green River

The lay of Utah's Green River, which enters the state from Wyoming, curves into Colorado and reenters the state, can be seen clearly in this aerial photograph taken from 32,000 feet. The point where it meets the Colorado River is at the bottom of the picture. On comparison, I began to wonder about names, because, at least at this point, this river is snakier than the Snake River in the Pacific Northwest. It was also interesting to note that this picture is just like a map. The distance between points at the top and bottom is 18.34 miles.

Rainbow River III

Calm and peaceful as it flows through the plain, it is hard to believe that the Rainbow River leveled land and forest on its journey down from the mountain. The dark spot at the upper right in the photograph—twenty miles distant—is the river's end, Illiuk Arm of Naknek Lake on the Alaska Peninsula. To pierce the ever-present fog, I used infrared film. The mountain at the upper left is Mount Katolinet, whose peak rises 4,728 feet, and the mountain at the right rises 4,175 feet. This is the side of the lake opposite the village of King Salmon.

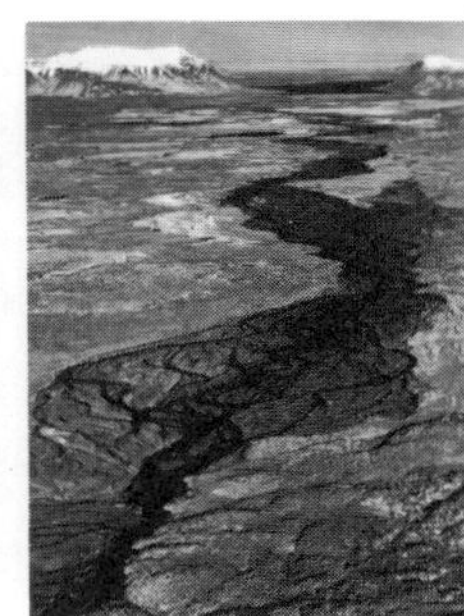

Valley of Ten Thousand Smokes

The eruption of Mount Novarupta and the collapse of Mount Katmai (from June 2 to 6, 1912) is believed to be one of the biggest volcanic disturbances in modern history. Not only was the valley covered to a depth of 700 feet by volcanic ash, but dust formed haze and spread, lowering temperatures in the Northern Hemisphere as far away as Europe and North Africa. River and hot spring water was gassified, leading Dr. Robert F. Griggs to give the valley its name four years later. At present, the mountain is calm, and there is little smoke in the valley.

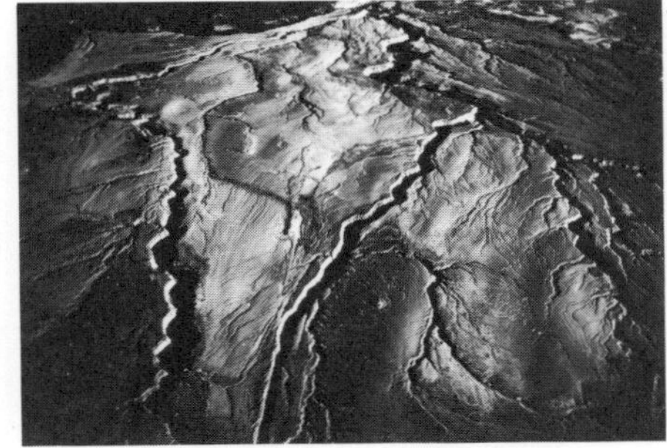

The Big Room

Located in the inner recesses of Carlsbad Caverns National Park in New Mexico, this is the biggest cavern there. At 285 feet, it has a height almost the same as the Capitol in Washington, D.C., and has enough room for fourteen football stadiums. One path runs around the cavern, but there is also a shortcut leading to the Temple of the Sun. The cavern is full of grotesquerie in the form of stalagmites and stalactites. The natural temperature is constant at about 56 degrees, which seems fairly warm in the winter but very chilly in the summer.

Bats I

It is recorded that when postbellum pioneers came here, they thought from a distance that they were seeing a column of smoke, but it turned out to be myriads of bats in flight. For thousands of years, millions and millions of bats have wintered in Mexico and spent the summer in Carlsbad Caverns' Bat Cave. These prehistoric mammals fly out in the evening to search for food. Concentration reaches a peak for a one-to-two week period in the middle of September. Revisiting the cave at that time, I took hundreds of pictures. This is one.

Bats II

Hanging down in daytime sleep, multitudes of bats blacken the ceiling of Bat Cave. Only the white places at the top and bottom of the picture are rock. The bats in flight are sentinels. The floor of the cave is covered with bat guano, and the odor, of course, is unpleasant. At one time, the guano was used for fertilizer, and it is said that 100,000 tons have been dug up and carried away, mostly to the citrus groves of California. We walked a considerable distance down from the entrance, then, using strobe flash, aimed our lenses at the 160-foot-high ceiling.

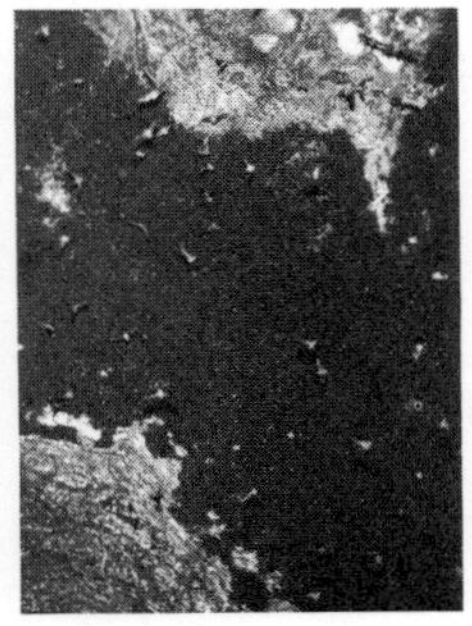

National Parks

Sigurd F. Olson

In 1973 some 200 million people visited the American National Parks System, a vast complex of 38 national parks, 87 national monuments, historic and archeological sites, recreational areas, wild and scenic rivers, and national trails, a total of 298 widely diverse regions comprising a cross section of the most beautiful and unique areas of this great country. A decade ago, visitation was only half what it is today, proof of the growing public interest and human need for the wild and unchanged parts of the land in which we live.

New reservations are constantly being created, not only in the spacious Far West but close to the metropolitan section of the East, as well as along the West Coast. There are millions of acres of wilderness within the national forests and wildlife refuges, and Congress has issued a mandate that over 83 million acres of Alaska's public domain be set aside for similar purposes to provide for the swiftly growing demand for open space and recreational use of our pyramiding population.

To visitors from foreign countries, it may seem as though this program of preserving wild and natural country in the highest public interest has always existed in our land and that therefore we should serve as a model for other less enlightened nations, but this is far from true, for it took a century or more to change the basic philosophy of a pioneer people, from one of conquering a hostile wilderness and exploiting its supposedly unlimited resources to make room for railroads, highways, towns and cities, to one of preservation of the land and recognition of its esthetic values. As Horace Albright, great authority on our national parks, said recently in speaking of this period, "It appears that industrial growth, agricultural expansion, public land homesteading, and timberland cutting were the prime public domain considerations of the American people."

The first intimations of any change in attitude came from such writers as Henry David Thoreau, Ralph Waldo Emerson, James Fenimore Cooper and others as well as from artists George Catlin, Albert Bierstadt and Thomas Moran in the eighteen hundreds, while the lands west of the Mississippi were still largely unexplored Indian country. From such voices emerged a belief that the wilderness scene might have some value besides the purely monetary one of exploitation and commercial use. Thoreau said, "In wilderness is the preservation of the world," and the painter George Catlin, "that vast areas should be set aside as natural preserves to be kept in its primitive condition for Indians, buffalo, and all indigenous forms of life to remind Americans of what the land was like before it was completely subdued." Few listened, however, to such outrageous ideas and the progress of destruction went on apace. Since the continent's discovery there has been only one goal: to push back the frontier no matter what the cost, with greed and the competitive spirit dominating not only government but people's minds. Great rewards went to the strong and ruthless, and no one thought there was any need to change our way of life or our view of the land itself.

Then an event occurred without precedent in our frontier history, largely due to John Muir and his great love of an area in California known as Yosemite, which included some of the groves of giant redwoods or Sequoia. The federal government ceded the tract to the newly formed State of California as a preserve. That law was signed by President Abraham Lincoln in 1864, an unheard of action and one criticized widely, but being the first it was an entering wedge into a pattern of thought that had dominated people's minds since our earliest occupancy of the Atlantic seaboard. It had a tremendous impact on our thinking and was a recognition of values hitherto unthought of, the idea that if this area was worth preserving there might be others as well.

One of these lands was the Yellowstone country northeast of the Yosemite, where strange and unique things were to be seen. Rumors had come from trappers, Indians and scouts of boiling hot springs, spouting geysers and hot steaming pools, of gorgeous mountains and lakes teeming with game, fur and fish, valleys of incomparable beauty and fertility. It became widely known as "Colter's Hell" because of the fantastic stories of one of the Mountain Men, and finally in 1870 due to growing public interest, an expedition was dispatched into the area to see if there was any basis of truth to the wild tales everyone had heard. The exploring party returned with equally fabulous accounts of what they had seen and were greeted by the usual suspicion and disbelief. The government, however, was now really curious, and a second expedition went in the following summer of 1871, this time with photographers, painters and scientists to bring out positive proof of what they had seen.

It was on this expedition that a miracle occurred that settled the fate of this region and of many others as well. All during this exploration there had been much discussion of what to do with the area, and it was mutually agreed it should be homesteaded and divided up and its wonders and resources sold to those who could exploit it and use it for profit, such as railroads and other developers.

But one night while camped on the Madison River, the group decided unanimously that because of the region's great and unusual features, it should not be exploited but set aside for the use and enjoyment of all Americans for all time. The report was scoffed at by Congress and the press, and the new philosophy held up to scorn as an insane and impractical concept. In spite of all, however, legislation was drawn up, and in 1872 some 2 million acres were set aside by Congress as Yellowstone National Park "for the use and enjoyment of the people."

Yosemite National Park was finally established by Congress in 1890 from the lands it had deeded to the State of California, but many years passed before full protection was given to either area. During this same period a drastic change in attitude was also manifesting itself in the East, in legislation by the State of New York setting aside some 750,000 acres of the beautiful cluster of mountains known as the Adirondacks as a forest preserve to be kept, according to the law of establishment, "Forever Wild." While this new concept was criticized and challenged again and again, a public referendum endorsed it overwhelmingly. Since then the overall area has grown to 6 million acres, and while there is much private land included in its boundaries, the area is protected by zoning regulations that it is hoped will preserve its beauty and character.

The pattern of public attitude was becoming firm, and in swift succession Mount Rainier was set aside as a national park in 1899, Crater Lake in 1902, Mesa Verde in 1906, Grand Canyon National Monument in 1908, Glacier National Park in 1910, Rocky Mountain National Park in 1915. By the time the National Park Service was created in 1916 to administer and protect the new reservations, a total of thirty-seven parks and monuments had been set aside with surveys going on in many other areas. The tide had finally turned and the famous National Park System was underway.

Around the turn of the century, President Theodore Roosevelt established many national forests and wildlife preserves in spite of the loud outcry against "locking up national lands from public use." To counter such criticism, he called a conference of governors in 1908 to explain his program and to endorse the establishment of the United States Forest Service in 1905. Many citizens groups were also present, and Horace McFarland, president of the American Civic Association, declared in support of the president's action, "The time has come to bring back the beauty of America. No one," he said, "will die for an ugly land but anyone will die for a beautiful one. Therefore the preservation of beauty is the highest form of patriotism." That was almost seventy years ago, but the public at last had become aware that the old pioneer philosophy of ruthless exploitation was coming to an end.

Now in 1975 the wilderness has been conquered, our population more than doubled until it seems at times there is no limit to the pyramiding of numbers. New cities are being spawned, and metropolitan ribbons reach from the major ones toward other huge complexes: New York west to Chicago and Milwaukee, Boston south along the Atlantic coast to Washington and the Carolinas, Miami along the Gulf of Mexico to New Orleans, and San Francisco south to Los Angeles along the Pacific Coast. More and more people are moving into such urban environments, removing themselves from the farms and small communities of the frontier of which they were so recently a part, a frontier that molded them as a people and left within them a longing and need for simplicity and naturalness they will not soon forget.

Our world today is faced with an energy shortage of serious proportions, and we are beginning to tear up the golden west to get at supplies of oil and coal and along our coastal shelves are embarked upon a tremendous and costly program of exploration. Our industrial system is grinding to a halt, and we wonder what to do with worldwide inflation, lack of goods and services. We are disturbed by unemployment, uncertainty, and changing habits of living, ethics, morals and religious faith. People are frustrated and bored with the purposeless lives they seem to be living and unhappy with the dehumanizing impact of automation and lack of reality in their world. They long for something missing that their forebears knew, something that gave color and challenge to an often hazardous and bitterly difficult existence. They yearn for simplicity, a change of scene from the tensions and clamor of urbanity, dream of the old frontier, though most of them would not return. Strangely, however, in this people the old pioneer philosophy is still rampant, and when the question of maintaining our economy and industrial base comes up and we move into beautiful areas for scarce resources, there is still the old refrain, "Why lock them up when needed for our way of life." There is even consideration of invading national parks and other reservations.

With the swift changes in world events, people at heart still turn intuitively to the realization that only in the stability of nature can they find a sense of balance and content, only through contact with influences that dominated their lives before the advent of technology can they find fulfillment. It makes little difference where they go or how far. They stream from the cities in constant search for what they have lost. Some travel thousands of miles to view the grandest and most spectacular of spectacles; others take short weekend excursions near their homes where they can catch for a moment glimpses of beauty and naturalness that mean perspective and spiritual renewal through their ancient ties to the earth.

What is this powerful need and why must we satisfy it? When the great historian Trevelyan said, "We are children of the earth and removed from her our spirits wither," he spoke for all mankind. We are still so close to our beginnings we cannot forget, no matter how sophisticated and affluent we have become. We still have need of periodic contact with the earth, and without opportunities to touch it now and then we lose our dignity and identity as men. Wild country, unspoiled lands, places of space and remoteness have become a spiritual necessity to the people of America. The hunger within them is not to be denied, and there is always a search for places where it can be appeased. We listen to the ancient song of the wilderness. As I once said, "I have discovered I am not alone in my listening, that almost everyone is listening for something; that the search for places where the singing of the wilderness can be heard goes on everywhere. It is part of the hunger all have for a time when we were closer to lakes, rivers, and forests than we are today. Because of our almost forgotten past there is a restlessness within us, an impatience with things as they are, which modern life with its comforts and distractions does not seem to satisfy. We sense intuitively that there is something more, search for panaceas that might give us a sense of reality, fill our days and nights with such activity and our minds with such busyness there is little time to think. When the pace stops, we are often lost and plunge once more into the maelstrom hoping that if we move fast enough, somehow we may fill the void within us. We may not know exactly what it is we are listening for but we hunt as instinctively for opportunities and places to listen as sick animals look for healing herbs."

"Even the search is rewarding, for somehow in the process we tap the deep wells of racial experience that give us a feeling of being part of an existence where life was simple and satisfactions deep and real. Uncounted centuries of the primitive have left their mark upon us and civilization has not changed emotional needs that were ours long before the dawn of history. This is the reason for the hunger and listening and constant search. Should we actually glimpse the ancient glory or hear the singing wilderness, cities and their confusion become places of quiet, speed and turmoil are slowed to the pace of the seasons, and tensions are replaced with calm."

John Masefield, poet laureate of England, in speaking of this sense of oneness with nature and of his own experience with what he called the greater life, said, "I believe that life to be the source of all that is of glory and goodness in the world and modern man not knowing that life is dwelling in death."

And so it has been with me in a lifetime of wilderness travel on this continent, especially through our national parks. Whenever I have renewed my sense of communion and belonging with the wild, whenever I have sensed even for an instant the glory Masefield speaks of, happiness and fulfillment have been mine. I feel I speak for countless millions all over the world who in their own way are searching for the same glory. I believe with Masefield that when we look at the earth and its beauties with awe and wonderment, we catch the meaning of our relationship to the universe, and when we do, the world of spirit and deep fulfillment is ours.

One has only to look at the long history of the human race to realize why this is so. A hundred thousand years have elapsed since the emergence of *Homo sapiens*, with vague beginnings running back perhaps two or three million years or more. The genetic background of eons of the primeval is woven inextricably into all of us with the great silences, timelessness and the inherent sense of being at one with all life.

We forget that only during the past thirty or forty thousand years did we develop any culture beyond that of the stone age or leave any evidence of cultural growth beyond the primitive paintings or pictographs on rock faces all over the world. Nor do we remember that only during the past five to seven thousand of those years did we leave any written historical record and, most significant of all, that only since the industrial revolution a couple of centuries ago did we change our lives by weaning ourselves from the earth and our ties with the past. The most astounding truth is that during the last few decades with an inventive genius that seems to have exploded in our minds, we have embarked on the greatest adventure of all, nuclear fission and the space age, holding in our hands the possibilities not only of destroying ourselves but the planet we call home. The machines by which we live, our missiles, with multinuclear warheads capable of the total decimation of cities and millions of people, and our antimissiles have added a new and horrible dimension to man's anxiety.

A strange and violent world is ours today, with the great silences replaced by the roar of jet engines and our enormous megalopolises vibrating with noise. The natural smells of fields and forests are replaced by those of combustion and industry, natural beauty by the pollution of air, soil and water and by the mounting ugliness of garbage and discarded debris. We have during these last decades changed the courses of rivers, leveled mountains, eroded the land, covered great areas with blacktop and concrete. We are changing climates and wind patterns, even our atmosphere to the point where solar radiation is so influenced that the earth may well become uninhabitable not only by us but by all life.

Men have walked on the moon and we have surrounded our planet with satellites for communication. With the additional advent of supersonic flight, no place on earth is isolated. We know more about the immensity of the universe and the structure of its most infinitesimal particles than we ever dreamed possible. We are probing ocean depths, learning the secrets of drifting continents, exploring solar, geothermal and nuclear energy to replace the sources we have exhausted during our phenomenally swift technological growth.

We have come a long way during the last few years, and one would think that with all we have done we should be the happiest humans this earth has ever known. We may think we have bridged the enormous gap between our present way of life and the past, but this is a fallacy. We have only to look at the high incidence of mental illness to know something is wrong. Man, unprepared for the machine age, is beset by a sense of incompleteness that nothing seems to satisfy. He tries desperately to make the adjustment not realizing that the key may be very simple: a return to the nature he once knew. His dilemma is ignorance of his past and the knowledge that complete adaptation never takes place easily or swiftly and that the guiding principle underlying human destiny is recognition of our own evolution and interrelationship with all living things on earth. If he would accept this, he could achieve balance and be content as part of an ancient community and so live at least in partial harmony with the land.

It is here that national parks play their greatest role, for people with their problems and needs are drawn intuitively toward them. When they search for something so fundamental to their spiritual well-being, knowing that nothing is more important than finding it; when they are in tune with wind, sea and sky and beauty everywhere, only then can they become whole.

Julian Huxley said it well: "One function of the earth whose importance we have only just begun to recognize is that of wilderness, the function of allowing men and women to get away from the complications of industrial civilization and make contact with scenery and unspoiled nature. In more general terms, the function of conserving nature is one to which we must assign a not inconsiderable area of the globe's surface."

In spite of warnings from the wise, far too small a part of the earth is so preserved. There must be much more, not only large expanses but smaller ones close to the cities where people can make them part of their daily lives rather than once every year or two on costly, time-consuming trips to far and exciting places. To put a value on any natural area, any park or historic landmark is as difficult as to place a value on an heirloom or a great poem. There are certain things that cannot be weighed on ordinary scales, for their value lies within the realm of the intangibles. Who can speak of the price of a Brahm's concerto, a Nefertiti or the realization of a dream fulfilled?

The value of national parks is in this category. While one might have great worth as a museum of natural phenomena, history or religious signficance, or for its unusual beauty, its real worth always depends on what it does to people's minds and hearts. If an area contributes in any way to spiritual well-being or provides a sense of filling the hunger and void within them, it enriches their lives and is beyond price.

Some find their solitude in tiny hidden corners, sometimes within the confines of cities themselves—a little glen or stand of trees, or a cluster of rocks where through accident or design, man has saved a breath of the primeval. Others crave distances and far horizons, vast reaches of unsettled wilderness where they know hunger and the weariness that comes after travel through difficult terrain. There are those who love the far north of the American continent, when after days of fighting gales, portaging, and running dangerous rapids, they find themselves a thousand miles from civilization on some unknown waterway; they know a satisfaction no other sanctuary can give. Those who know the mountains feel a similar joy. When camped in some high alpine meadow above timberline with gleaming snowclad peaks all around, they feel the primeval on a noble scale, for this to them is the ultimate of immensity and space. There are many who feel that only in the great swamplands and flowages of the south, in the Everglades, the flooded cypress stands, or along the deltas and savannas of semitropical rivers and swamps can they really understand what wilderness means, for in such places life evolved.

Whatever their type or wherever they are found, on this continent or any place in the world, such areas fill a vital need as a balance wheel and spiritual backlog to the high-speed mechanical world in which we live. It is not surprising, therefore, that when urban living and its synthetic pleasures fail to satisfy, people turn intuitively toward these last reserves to catch the mystery of the unknown and the beauty of what is still primeval.

While it is doubtful that our ancestors appreciated the intangible values of wild country, we moderns are beginning to. Today we understand that within it are the secrets of sanity and equlibrium in our troubled world, realizing that wonder and beauty have always been and always will be the wellsprings of cultural progress just as they were in the past.

Beauty never stands alone but is a composite of the great silences and blue horizons that give a peace of mind beyond understanding. Beauty embodies the hopes and dreams of all who have gone before. It includes the spirit world and all perception and is so fragile it can be destroyed by a careless action or a foreign thought. It can be infinitesimally small or encompass the universe itself. It can come in a glance wherever nature has not been disturbed. National parks are museums of beauty. John Galsworthy said: "It is the contemplation of beautiful visions which slowly generation by generation has lifted man to his present state. Nothing in the world but the love of beauty in its broadest sense stands between man and the full and reckless exercise of his competitive greed."

Here alone is justification for national parks anywhere in the world, for within them are many of the planet's most beautiful scenes. Before them moderns sense the visions that stirred our forebears, visions that have always played a powerful role in the creative genius of the human mind and the calming of the human spirit.

Over the centuries a host of perceptive men have believed that if man saw his true relationship to the earth and the universe, he could become part of the order and reason governing his existence, the movement of galaxies as well as the minutest divisions of matter. Bertrand Russell affirmed this thought when he said: "It is possible to live in so large a world that the vexations of daily life come to feel trivial and the purposes which stir our deeper emotions take on something of the immensity of cosmic contemplation. If man can acquire this kind of wisdom, our new powers over nature offer a prospect of happiness and well-being such as men have never known before."

That perhaps is what the ancient Greek meant when he said that "life is a gift of nature and a beautiful life a gift of wisdom."

This much is true: the stature of man has increased because of beauty and harmony and the challenge of mystery, not through the ugliness of warped and twisted psychosis. It is just as true that physical ugliness about us does affect our attitudes and happiness. In fact the two are so closely intertwined it is impossible to speak of one without considering the other. The real cause of our discontent with things as they are is that we have severed our spiritual roots.

Today as never before we need wisdom not only to solve the many complexities of life but those inner frustrations that come from the dehumanizing impact of a way of life enmeshed in mass production and automation in a machine age. In the development of any program for either the destruction or the protection of natural areas, we must ask ourselves whether or not we care enough about their true value to make the sacrifices necessary to protect and hold them for a higher use, the preservation of humanity itself.

This is a time for major decisions: whether, for example, it is right morally or ethically to destroy entire river systems for hydropower, irrigation or mining, with the violation and irrevocable changing of entire ecosystems. We may be asked to consider using the famous geysers of Yellowstone for geothermal power or damming its great falls or those of the Colorado to provide the enormous amounts of water for oil and shale development in the Southwest. Will we destroy the last great wilderness of Alaska with multiple corridors for roads and pipelines in the far north? These are but a few of the questions we must consider during the next decade, for no part of the continent is so removed or inaccessible that it will not be studied in trying to solve the overriding problems of our technological system and its economy.

What we decide may well determine the future of mankind and perhaps his very survival. That coupled with the insanity of the nuclear arms race and the possibility of ending all life in a cataclysmic instant of horror add an urgency and threat mankind has never faced before.

It is always easy to allow political or economic pressures to take precedence over such nebulous considerations as beauty and spiritual welfare, and there will always be those who would exploit the national parks for gain if it would further their personal aggrandizement toward power. It behooves us, therefore, to look long and searchingly at any proposals, no matter how logical and desirable they may appear at the moment, that could change the quality of our lives by destroying the character of the land that contributes so much to humanitarian welfare. In the act establishing the National Parks System, Congress pledged itself to pass on unimpaired the areas entrusted to its care. This can be done if the people as a whole understand fully their significance. Only then can such places of inspiration stand inviolate for all time.

The existence of the present National Parks System is proof of a growing appreciation of its value, but we must not forget there is always danger in the attitudes of those who are more concerned with continued growth of industry than human values. "Surely," say the economic experts, "we can produce all we need for the coming billions and with our technology find ways of supplanting dwindling natural resources until the end of this century."

There is some truth in what they say, but the question still remains: is this enough, is it enough to live on a bare subsistence level, and does not man require more than food, modern gadgets and housing? Does he not require nourishment of the spirit as well, and is not a higher quality of life the all-important consideration? The population explosion together with burgeoning industrialization, not only in the so-called developed nations but in those that look forward to the affluence we have enjoyed, complicates the situation everywhere, for we are bound together in a common cause. No country but looks forward to the kind of life technology can provide. Peoples who are starving in many regions ask for help from wealthy nations, but this takes added energy, fertilizers, transportation and scarce resources. We are caught in a dilemma not easily solved, with international pressures mounting for the opening up of reserves everywhere. In the days to come we will be driven as never before to satisfy the physical needs not only of our own people but of those in the rest of the world not as fortunate as we. We must act with wisdom and courage. No greater decision faces us today, for in our choices we see the road we must follow.

While preserving the final remnants of Eternal America may seem only one facet of our problems, it indicates our attitude toward life and its true meaning. If we have the courage and vision to protect what we have and even set aside additional lands while there is still time, we will be acting in accordance with mankind's profoundest needs. While our national parks and other wilderness preserves may seem adequate today, they will not be able to fulfill the demands of the future. Unless we increase them substantially and keep them absolutely inviolate, generations to come will never know what we have known. As Luther Gulick, the great city planner, once said: "We will need new concepts of recreation and living space guided by our new psychological knowledge matched to urban life and the changing life patterns of our people. We need active programs for some, contemplative opportunities for many, and glimpses of beauty for all within the confines of the urban design itself."

Since that fateful day in 1872 when Yellowstone National Park was established, setting in motion a new thought pattern for Americans, the system has grown, and we are inordinately proud that our example may have influenced other nations in setting up preserves and parklands in many parts of the world. The International Union for the Protection of Nature meeting in Nairobi in 1974 stressed the identification of potential park areas in many countries. The United Nations' list of such areas, compiled in 1973 according to Kai Curry Lindahl, totals 978 in 72 countries, which will form a basis for the future of an expanded global network of parks furthered by the hope for establishment of The World Heritage Trust to safeguard for all time outstanding natural environments under the guidance of the United Nations.

Mr. Lindahl in a recent lecture in Washington quoted a message from the president of the United States during the Congress on Environment in 1971 that sums up the hope of the world in protecting and creating national parks everywhere.

"Confronted with the pressures of population and development, and with the world's tremendous capacity for environmental modification, we must act together to save for future generations the most outstanding natural areas as well as places of unique historical, archeological, architectural and of cultural value to mankind."

During the time I served as president of the National Parks Association of America, I was in touch with leaders in Japan working toward similar goals in their own country. Since those days Japan has accomplished much in the face of the tremendous odds of limited space, an inspiration to all nations of what can be done if the will and the vision are there. I treasure the mutual friendships that resulted from working together with Japanese leaders in this field.

It is an honor I deeply appreciate being asked to write this essay for *Eternal America*, with its beautiful photographs of American national parks by the great artist Yoshikazu Shirakawa. I am confident the book will contribute greatly toward their preservation over the crucial years ahead and cement even more firmly a mutual interest begun long ago. With its dramatic and unusual interpretation, it will make our people more aware and appreciative of what they have, and I am sure it will have a similar impact in other countries and will strengthen the growing conviction that parks everywhere must be protected for all time as living symbols of the truth that man cannot live by bread alone.

During an address before the first International Parks Conference held in Seattle in 1962, I said:

"We in America believe our national parks play an important role in providing glimpses of beauty for all and hope it will be that way for all time to come. We cherish them for what they mean and believe in them because we know what they contribute to human happiness. We are pledged to preserve them no matter how difficult it may become. What we have done has been possible only because our people believed they were worthwhile. I have faith in the future that the same conviction that has supported the parks in the past seventy odd years will remain unshaken. If the great numbers of Americans making a pilgrimage each year to them is any indication of their concern, then in spite of threats they will survive."

Since then there have been other international conferences in many parts of the world, all of them stressing the need for nations everywhere to establish reservations of their own. Out of it has come the endorsement of the United Nations, the hope of an international World Heritage Trust dedicated to the cause of furthering the ideal of a planetary system of national parks.

Eternal America will bolster the resolve of those in all nations who now have the vision and it may open the eyes of those who are still unaware.

Shigene Kanamaru

While I was still active as a professor of photography at Nihon University in Tokyo, Yoshikazu Shirakawa was one of my students. It is only natural for a teacher to wonder what life holds in store for his students. In Shirakawa's case, I believe he has not only succeeded in his chosen profession but has gone on to excel, becoming a pioneer in the art of photography.

As one climbs the Himalayas, how small, like ants, do the people in the foothills appear. When I once stood atop Tiger Hill and viewed the distant, magnificent Kangchenjunga, a tremor of awe ran through my body, leaving me speechless. But a thunderstruck person cannot use a camera. Shirakawa sometimes takes a conventional picture, engaging in the poetic reflection of a moon hanging over a towering peak, but this is not typical. He usually aims his camera at the realities of the earth, the grandeur and colossal strength that are nature's own. He views nature's beauty with a cool, discerning eye.

His masterpieces of mountains give the impression of being more massive than the originals. In capturing their splendor and ruggedness, he adds a dimension. The bigger and grander the object, the more he tackles it with his boundless energy.

The spirit of nature lies in the solemnity and mysteriousness inherent in it. It is for the photographer to draw this spirit out of nature. With his undaunted spirit, Shirakawa is admirably adept at his work, for his will and enthusiasm are never dampened. The greatness of the man is evident in all his works, and he fits perfectly in the world of photography, where the most minute expression is the penultimate.

His works are far too numerous to catalogue here, but take, for example, his photograph of Mount Kangtega, a lesser peak. He captures with uncompromising accuracy each and every rocky crevice of the mountainside, his assessment of what the mountain is piercing our hearts like a dagger. Space, time: he expresses one as well as the other, as in his photographs of Mount McKinley's glaciers, where we see time at a virtual standstill pulsating with life.

In the Alps and the Himalayas, the feeling is of perpendicularity, of the earth rising. In his photography of the American continent, Shirakawa has explored an additional dimension, that of horizontality, which gives the feeling of unlimited space, changing in accordance with natural conditions—the seasons, the time of day, the weather. Before this book was published, I spent two days looking over the selection of photographs. It was an astounding experience. I recalled seeing a picture of the earth taken from Apollo 10 and thinking how strange it was that I was standing on that very earth. There are many photographs in *Eternal America* that give rise to that same feeling of strangeness, for no one has ever taken ones like this before.

What is the source of Shirakawa's boundless energy? Born in 1935, he spent an uneventful childhood in Ehime Prefecture on the island of Shikoku, but life became difficult during his years in college. That was during the 1950s, the economy was in a state of recession, and his father, a maker of the traditional Japanese paper known as *washi*, could no longer offer his financial support. Shirakawa persevered, supporting himself with a variety of part-time jobs, ranging from delivery boy to work on a weekly photographic newspaper, and managed to graduate—barely.

As an alpine photographer, he found his first job as a television cameraman difficult to adjust to, yet he succeeded in publishing his maiden effort, *Shiroi Yama*, or "White Mountains," in 1960. What attracted wide attention was a series of three photographs of the Hakkōda Mountains—the superb evocation of the surface of the slopes, the contrast of shadows, and the stimulating freshness resulting from the use of wide-angle lenses. The techniques noted today for their excellence had already appeared in his first efforts. From then on, he chose rather than mountains as a whole only portions of them viewed from his individualistic angle and showing their abstract form.

Figuratively, he has climbed other mountains as well, seeking out the heights attained by other top photographers of the world: Vittoria Sella, who was the only photographer of the Roof of the World before Shirakawa published the *Himalayas*, and Edward Weston and Ansel Adams, extraordinary photographers of their own land, for whom he has deep respect. I feel that Shirakawa has taken a great leap forward and that his collections will no doubt leave an indelible imprint on the history of photography. It is interesting to note that Edward Hoagland, reviewing the *Himalayas* in the *New York Times* wrote, "He is undoubtedly the world's bravest outdoor artist, and if we were to try to hit upon a man to obtain a picture of God, it would need to be Shirakawa."

Fifteen trips to the Alps proceeded the publication of *The Alps* in 1969, and four years were spent in the mountains before publication of the *Himalayas*, which brought him worldwide fame.

Arnold Toynbee in his preface to the latter book writes, "The splendour that shines through Nature is imparted to her from a source which is beyond Nature and which is the ultimate reality." Toynbee, however, also directs sharply barbed criticism against modern civilization, which is destroying nature. Sharing this view, Shirakawa has sought to define his own philosophy of nature and humanity and advocates not only the rediscovery of this earth of ours but, through that, the rehabilitation of the human heart.

His ultimate purpose, it seems to me, lies in showing to the people the wonderful beauties of nature, which they can seldom see, and instilling in them a greater understanding of the glories of the world. He may seem a romanticist, but this is exactly the reason he has been successful in realizing his objective. A man of lesser conviction could not possibly have lived through the perils he confronted during his photographic sojourn in America, nor could a photographer of lesser stature have taken his masterpieces of Eternal America. And, as with men in many walks of life, it must be remembered that the difficulties and hardships he overcame during his youthful days have no doubt contributed much to make him what he is today.

Over a period of sixteen years, I have made photographic trips to 130 of the world's conutries, seeing with my own eyes, I believe, nearly all of nature's wonderful creations and developing a worldwide point of view. I have photographed from the ground and from the air, my flights having numbered in the thousands, and feel that I am accustomed to seeing nature as a macrocosm.

The scenic spots of this world are uncountable—the fjords of Norway, the glaciers of Iceland, the beautiful blue South Pacific, the Sahara, and many, many others. Nothing has impressed me more than the Alps, for nothing touches their wonderous beauty. Words fail to describe the view of Mont Blanc from Lac Blanc—the highest of the Alps touching the sky, the Aiguille du Dru and Grandes Jorasses glistening in purple to the left, the clouds swiftly flowing, turning red, purple, yellow. Sitting by the lake and watching the swiftly changing sky and mountains, I was oblivious to the passage of time until I became aware of the darkness that enveloped me.

As I rose to go down the mountain, I saw the moon rising over the north wall of the Grandes Jorasses. Immobile, I stood in a world of blue silence, gazing at the mountains until the moon was high in the sky.

In the early morning, the view of the Matterhorn from Lake Liffel was magnificent. The rising sun burned sky and clouds golden, and the rays striking the eastern wall of the mountain burnished it crimson. I felt pierced to the quick by the flames of the sun. It was as if I had been struck on the head by a thick oaken staff and momentarily lost consciousness, so soul shaking was the experience.

Alpine photography was not my interest at first, but I believe I have come to understand the reason. When I was still young, my imagination of photogenic objects was already replete with color, but the mountain photographs that I saw were lusterless and drab, shorn of the crimson, the blue, the golden colors that greeted my own eyes when I made that first trip. In a fleeting moment, I became enamored of the mountains, and from that day I took their pictures over a period of nine years.

Later I took my next step, capturing the rugged beauty of the Himalayas with my camera. There are fourteen peaks over twenty-six thousand feet, three hundred over twenty-two thousand feet and peaks over nineteen thousand feet too numerous to count. In the dry season, which is winter, the cold at an elevation of nineteen thousand feet is indescribable. With the jet stream blowing up from the Tibetan side, temperatures crash, but the peaks come to life in this frozen air.

The pink glow strikes Everest first, gradually spreads to the lesser peaks of Lhotse and Makalu. Suddenly the pace quickens, and the sun's rays cover the whole of the Himalayas, lifting them from a world of gray to one brilliantly colorful and full of life. The peaks seem to get higher and higher. Witnessing this sight at the break of dawn was an experience that at first I could not believe. So spectacular was the scene that unfolded before my eyes that I thought it a netherworld.

To speak of the "mysteries" and "wonders" of nature is easy, but I wonder how many people have felt the meaning of those words. How many people have actually experienced those mysteries and those wonders? Very few, I imagine. I feel fortunate in believing that I am one of the few, and it is my earnest wish to pass on to all my deep impressions and barely imaginable experiences. I would like them to discover anew this earth of ours. It is my fervent desire to show the way to a revitalization of humanity through the pictures I have taken.

Our age cries, as no other period in the history of mankind has, for the rekindling of the human conscience. Space scientists, medical scientists have taken great strides and made great contributions to mankind; technological advances pile up at a dizzying rate. Yet there is domestic unrest, there are wars between nations, and even in times of peace we are ruining our environment. Day by day our earth is being destroyed, and I have had the fear that in doing my work I may inadvertently have added a stroke to the blueprint of a plan that would make the earth desertic, uninhabitable.

Eternal America is the third of my photo albums urging rediscovery of the earth. Feeling that the country is a patient in critical condition, on the verge of death, I have been critical of America, where presidents and peace leaders and others have been assassinated. Notwithstanding the social conditions, I have come to this work with the sole purpose of showing the grandeur of nature in the United States, the only country in the world where one can see nature in its pristine state. Moreover, I evaluate highly the meticulous way the United States is planning to preserve nature for posterity. I was deeply impressed by the organization and effort directed toward safeguarding the country's natural beauty.

When, some 4.6 billion years ago, this earth was formed, it was covered with volcanic gases; then came oxygen, air and water, and plant life appeared on the surface of the earth.

The Kaibab Plateau has known the bite of the Colorado River for a million years, and the Grand Canyon was created. The sand of Colorado's Great Sand Dunes, the largest of their kind, also dates from a million years ago. And it was around a million years ago that man appeared. What was the earth like in the days of the dim past?

At least until recently, man's relationship to nature has been a close one, and since ancient days, philosophers and scientists have said that man's progress, which has been great, has been achieved because of his deep admiration and respect for nature. It was this spirit of respect for nature that has made man what he is today. But man in his material existence can have no pride.

Concealed in nature's depths is something that transcends anything material. It is this that I have sought to reproduce in all my photographs of mountains and canyons, rivers and glaciers . . .

In America, nature is all but boundless in its vastness. One hopes that is it impossible to destroy Alaska's plateaus or the deserts of Nevada and Arizona. It is easy to destroy. It is not easy to create. Energy and will are not themselves sufficient.

Recovery of humanity through rediscovery of the earth is my lifelong theme. *The Alps, Himalayas, Eternal America*, are now in book form. In the future, I want to look at the Andes and Patagonia, fjords, one hundred famous mountains of the world and the Japanese Alps. My lifework was planned thirteen years ago; I do not know whether I can accomplish my aim. My hope is to introduce to the world the not yet unraveled mysteries of nature. If through my photographs people were to rediscover this earth of ours, my joy could know no bounds.

Notes on Photography

For my first two books, I chose mountains as the subject with which to illustrate my theme. This time I chose a continent, for clearly imprinted on it are the evolutionary processes of 4.6 billion years. Eternal earth, great earth, Mother Earth: the definition varies according to the philosophy of the definer. What is unambiguous is that the photographer must have a philosophy.

For black and white photography, I used only infrared film, for it reveals things far beyond the range of the human eye. This type of film is used for alpine photography but rarely for more common scenes. I found it very effective for aerial photography and was startled at the details, such as roads and observation platforms, that came out sharply when the film was enlarged. That, of course, was my objective. I wanted to depict in two pages an area of several hundred square miles with all its configurations and disfigurations—canyons, plateaus, deserts, rivers, lakes.

Another reason for the infrared film was the inspiration I had derived from Edward Weston's photographs of Death Valley and Ansel Adams's pictures of Yosemite. They are masterpieces, and I admire both men greatly. However, had I set out to take pictures the same as theirs, there would have been little point in my spending fifteen months in the United States. In a word, their works were not only an inspiration but a challenge.

Since I could not obtain the infrared film of my choice in the United States, I purchased a supply of Sakura infrared film in Japan and used that. All color film, Kodak Ektachrome Professional, was purchased in the United States.

I had all film processed in Japan, having been advised by a friend who was working in a color laboratory in the United States that photo processing there was not up to par. And I found this to be true. On opening an envelope of black and white film developed in Los Angeles, I was left speechless. The negatives were not enclosed in individual holders, and they had been trimmed to the length of the envelope. Thereafter, all film was mailed to Japan.

The cameras I used were: three Asahi Pentax 6-by-7 cm and two Asahi Pentax ES. Most pictures were taken with the 6-by-7.

The lenses I took with me were (for the 6-by-7-cm camera body):

SMC Takumar fisheye	f/4.5, 35 mm	SMC Takumar	f/4, 200 mm
SMC Takumar	f/3.5, 55 mm	SMC Takumar	f/4, 300 mm
SMC Takumar	f/4.5, 75 mm	Takumar	f/4, 600 mm
SMC Takumar	f/2.4, 105 mm	Takumar	f/4, 800 mm

I also took three converters.

As I have said elsewhere, America is vast. In the desert, I could not tell whether a hill was six or sixty miles away. The ordinary combination of a 35-mm camera with a 100-mm or 135-mm telephoto lens was useless for my purposes. This was also true of wide-angle lenses, there being virtually no difference between photographs taken with them, nor any significant difference between photographs taken with either one of them and those taken with an ordinary lens. With a fisheye lens, I could finally see the difference from the angle of distortion apparent in the picture. It is indeed difficult to depict nature in the wide-open spaces of the United States.

To the naked eye, the Grand Canyon or Yosemite is a grand sight, but with either an ordinary or a fisheye lens, a picture taken from the South Rim shows only a small flat image of a plain wall. It is like taking a picture of a model. It is a fact that small scenes make better photographic subjects than great nature, and I feel that this is the reason that American photographers chose the small sand dunes of Death Valley in preference to those of the Great Sand Dunes. To catch nature in its greatness, I took pictures in the morning and the evening when the weather is variable, using fisheye lenses for the first time. I used a 600-mm telephoto lens, sometimes with an 8x converter, to take several thousand pictures.

Natural conditions sometimes hampered my efforts. In the desert in the summer, there were blinding sandstorms, and of course sand got into my cameras; I had to cover them with plastic. And though we disassembled and cleaned our tripods every day, after a few weeks they were useless and had to be replaced. While photographing Mount Whitney, my cameras stopped working suddenly, the batteries weakened by the intense cold. After that, I kept the battery in an inside pocket, but near the Arctic Circle I had another problem. Apparently a bit of saliva got inside the camera, froze in the subzero weather, and blocked the contact point.

Our primary transportation was a camper purchased in Los Angeles, in which we traveled 22,690 miles. We also used rental cars and jeeps to cover 7,980 miles and, particularly for places inaccessible by vehicle, airplanes, two hundred flights totaling nearly six hundred hours. We visited forty-one places, some of them three times, making fifty-five visits altogether.

I made a point of always photographing scenes straight from the front in order to obtain width and depth.

In a letter to me, Arnold Toynbee once said that a photograph is a record and its excellence depends on whether it is a moving record. His words are based on realism, but that itself is a poor word. Unless the emotions and philosophy of the cameraman are in his works, a print from a camera is little different from a xerox copy of it.

No other medium of expression compares with the camera. I cannot but dislike pictures taken out of focus or using other stagey effects in an attempt to imitate music, painting or poetry. Neither evoking deep feeling nor aspiring to a high spiritual level, they inevitably fail. A sharp, clear photograph expresses poetic feeling. Any expression not in pursuit of the human spirit is nothing to me.

A comparison of a picture of the Matterhorn with Richard Strauss's *Alpen Symphony,* or any number of photographs of the Grand Canyon with Ferde Grofé's *Grand Canyon,* is an exercise in futility and nothing more. A photograph is a photograph and nothing else. This was my principle when I took pictures for *Eternal America.*

Acknowledgments

A composer or painter can travel great distances on imagination alone, but a photographer cannot; he must be comparatively close to his subject. For me to penetrate the wilderness of nature without assistance was impossible. And since I was in a foreign country, there were complications arising from the differences in language, customs and law. Without the kindness and cooperation of a great number of people, my photographic objectives could not have been fulfilled. I would like to express my profound gratitude to the following persons who have done so much to promote whatever success my venture may enjoy.

Fred M. Packard, International Specialist, National Park Service, U.S. Department of the Interior

Edward F. Pilley, Jr., National Park Service, Western District

John Tunney, Superintendent, White Sands National Monument

Hugh Borsaz, Chief Ranger, White Sands National Monument

Phillip Van Clive, Chief of Technical Services, Carlsbad Caverns National Park

Charles Peterson, Ranger, Carlsbad Caverns National Park

Susan Cowles, Ranger, Carlsbad Caverns National Park

Charles A. Veitl, Superintendent, Petrified Forest National Park

Merle E. Stitt, Superintendent, Grand Canyon National Park

Leonard Frank, Ranger, Grand Canyon National Park

Roy Cry, Ranger, Monument Valley Navajo Tribal Park

Glen Alexander, Chief Ranger, Canyonlands and Arches National Parks

Stanley Albright, Alaska State Director, National Park Service

James Ritter, Specialist in Interpretive Management

Don Sheldon, Talkeetna Air Service

James Lucy, Ranger, Katmai National Monument

Charles V. Janda, Chief Ranger, Glacier Bay National Monument

Elder Kenneth at Glacier Bay Lodge

King Riley, Riley's Flying Service, Green Sea of Dunes, Nebraska

James Sleznick, Ranger, Yosemite National Park

Don H. Castleberry, Superintendent, Timpanogos Cave National Monument

John Crumblink, Interpretive Officer, Lava Beds National Monument

Richard J. Munro, Management Assistant, Glacier National Park

James Calico, Superintendent, Great Sand Dunes National Monument

David Ziegler, Deputy Chief, Tokyo Branch, Department of Commerce Tourist Bureau

Yasuko Gamō, Tokyo Branch, Department of Commerce Tourist Bureau

Sumiko Inoue, Information Officer, Tokyo Branch, Department of Commerce Tourist Bureau

Nobuhiko Ushiba, former Japanese ambassador to the United States

Hisahiko Okazaki, First Secretary, Embassy of Japan, Washington, D.C.

Koten Hibino, Manager, Passenger Department Japan, Pan American Airlines

Mitsuo Agishi, Los Angeles Liaison Office

Akiko Agishi, Los Angeles Liaison Office

Tadao Kimura and the staff of Musiphone

Hisatsune Sakomizu, Member of the House of Councillors, National Diet of Japan

Staff of the Cultural Affairs Bureau, Ministry of Foreign Affairs

Saburō Matsumoto, President, Asahi Optical Co., Ltd.

Hiroshi Hara, Executive Director, Asahi Optical Co., Ltd.

Shigenobu Hieda, Publicity Manager, Asahi Optical Co., Ltd.

Nobuo Mogi, Publicity Manager, Konishiroku Photo Industry, Ltd.

Mitsutsuna Kuchiki, Konishiroku Photo Industry, Ltd.

This book is a work made possible by the cooperative efforts of two countries, the United States and Japan, and through the friendship and trust existing between the persons whose names appear above and myself. My deepest gratitude to all those who have extended their kind cooperation to me.

Maps

AMERICA
Location of Photography

NATIONAL PARKS & NATIONAL MONUMENTS

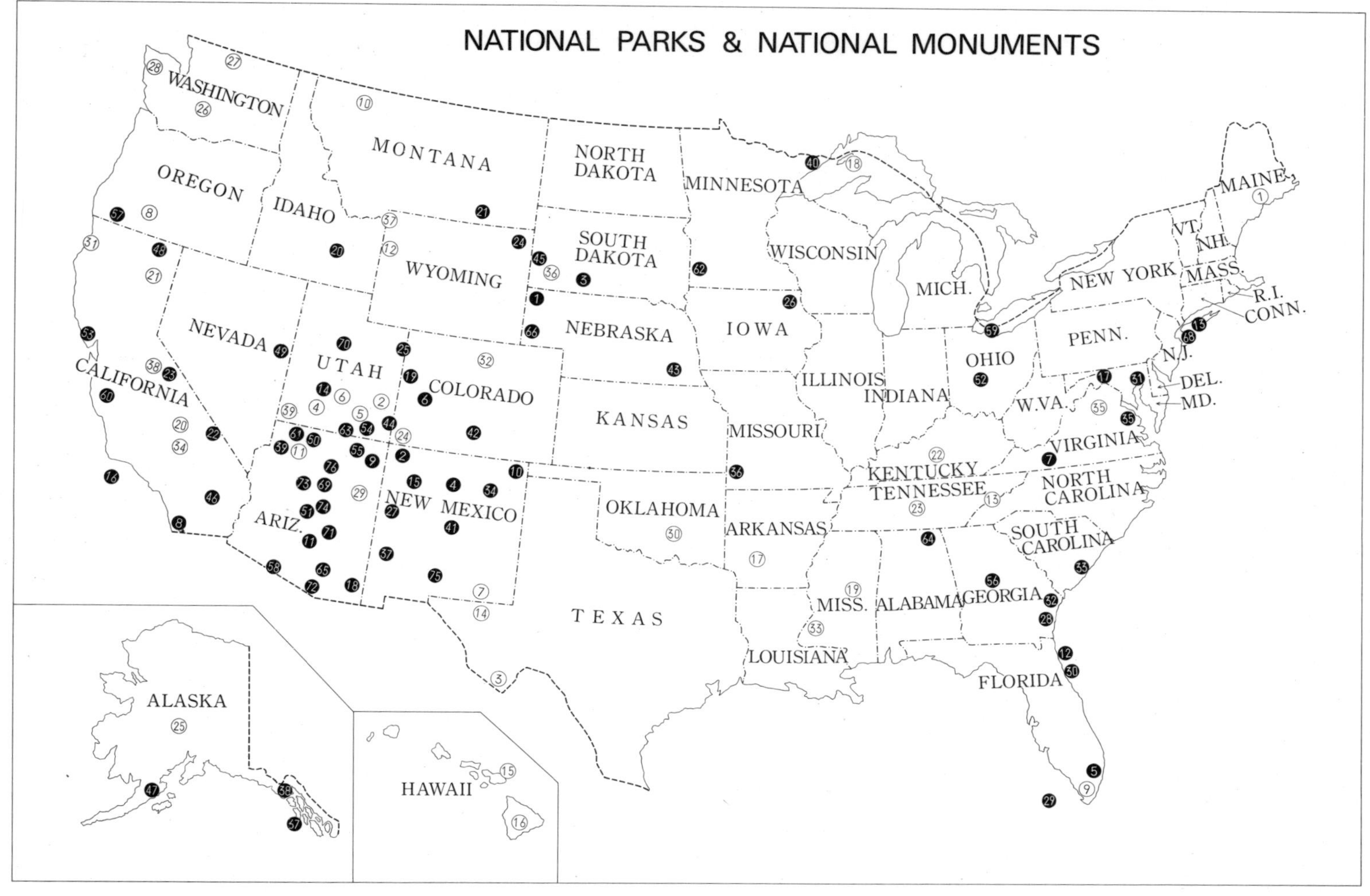

NATIONAL PARKS

			sq. mi. (approx.)
①	Acadia	Maine	65
②	Arches	Utah	130
③	Big Bend	Texas	1107
④	Bryce Canyon	Utah	56
⑤	Canyonlands	Utah	403
⑥	Capitol Reef	Utah	397
⑦	Carlsbad Caverns	New Mexico	73
⑧	Crater Lake	Oregon	250
⑨	Everglades	Florida	2188
⑩	Glacier	Montana	1583
⑪	Grand Canyon	Arizona	1052
⑫	Grand Teton	Wyoming	485
⑬	Great Smoky Mountains	N. Carolina & Tenn.	805
⑭	Guadalupe Mountains	Texas	121
⑮	Haleakala	Hawaii	41
⑯	Hawaii Volcanoes	Hawaii	344
⑰	Hot Springs	Arkansas	6
⑱	Isle Royale	Michigan	843
⑲	Jeff Busby	Mississippi	†
⑳	Kings Canyon	California	719
㉑	Lassen Volcanic	California	167
㉒	Mammoth Cave	Kentucky	80
㉓	Meriwether Lewis	Tennessee	†
㉔	Mesa Verde	Colorado	81
㉕	Mount McKinley	Alaska	3030
㉖	Mount Rainier	Washington	378
㉗	North Cascades	Washington	789
㉘	Olympic	Washington	1401
㉙	Petrified Forest	Arizona	147
㉚	Platt	Oklahoma	1
㉛	Redwood	California	91
㉜	Rocky Mountain	Colorado	410
㉝	Rocky Springs	Mississippi	†
㉞	Sequoia	California	604
㉟	Shenandoah	Virginia	302
㊱	Wind Cave	South Dakota	44
㊲	Yellowstone	Wyo., Mon. & Idaho	3472
㊳	Yosemite	California	1190
㊴	Zion	Utah	230

NATIONAL MONUMENTS

❶	Agate Fossil Beds	Nebraska	†
❷	Aztec Ruins	New Mexico	*
❸	Badlands	South Dakota	174
❹	Bandelier	New Mexico	43
❺	Biscayne	Florida	†
❻	Black Canyon of the Gunnison	Colorado	21
❼	Booker T. Washington	Virginia	*
❽	Cabrillo	California	*
❾	Canyon de Chelly	Arizona	131
❿	Capulin Mountain	New Mexico	1
⓫	Casa Grande Ruins	Arizona	1
⓬	Castillo de San Marcos	Florida	*
⓭	Castle Clinton	New York	*
⓮	Cedar Breaks	Utah	10
⓯	Chaco Canyon	New Mexico	34
⓰	Channel Islands	California	28
⓱	Chesapeake & Ohio Canal	Maryland & W. Virginia	7
⓲	Chiricahua	Arizona	17
⓳	Colorado	Colorado	27
⓴	Craters of the Moon	Idaho	84
㉑	Custer Battlefield	Montana	1
㉒	Death Valley	California & Nevada	2981
㉓	Devils Postpile	California	1
㉔	Devils Tower	Wyoming	2
㉕	Dinosaur	Utah & Colorado	322
㉖	Effigy Mounds	Iowa	2
㉗	El Morro	New Mexico	2
㉘	Fort Frederica	Georgia	*
㉙	Fort Jefferson	Florida	74
㉚	Fort Matanzas	Florida	*
㉛	Fort McHenry	Maryland	*
㉜	Fort Pulaski	Georgia	9
㉝	Fort Sumter	South Carolina	*
㉞	Fort Union	New Mexico	1
㉟	George Washington's Birthplace	Virginia	1
㊱	George Washington Carver	Missouri	*
㊲	Gila Cliff Dwellings	New Mexico	1
㊳	Glacier Bay	Alaska	4381
㊴	Grand Canyon	Arizona	310
㊵	Grand Portage	Minnesota	1
㊶	Gran Quivira	New Mexico	1
㊷	Great Sand Dunes	Colorado	57
㊸	Homestead	Nebraska	*
㊹	Hovenweep	Utah and Colorado	1
㊺	Jewel Cave	South Dakota	2
㊻	Joshua Tree	California	872
㊼	Katmai	Alaska	4366
㊽	Lava Beds	California	72
㊾	Lehman Caves	Nevada	1
㊿	Marble Canyon	Arizona	41
(51)	Montezuma Castle	Arizona	1
(52)	Mound City Group	Ohio	*
(53)	Muir Woods	California	1
(54)	Natural Bridges	Utah	12
(55)	Navajo	Arizona	1
(56)	Ocmulgee	Georgia	1
(57)	Oregon Caves	Oregon	1
(58)	Organ Pipe Cactus	Arizona	517
(59)	Perry's Victory & Int'l Peace Memorial	Ohio	*
(60)	Pinnacles	California	23
(61)	Pipe Spring	Arizona	*
(62)	Pipestone	Minnesota	*
(63)	Rainbow Bridge	Utah	*
(64)	Russell Cave	Alabama	*
(65)	Saguaro	Arizona	123
(66)	Scotts Bluff	Nebraska	5
(67)	Sitka	Alaska	*
(68)	Statue of Liberty	New York	*
(69)	Sunset Crater	Arizona	5
(70)	Timpanogos Cave	Utah	*
(71)	Tonto	Arizona	2
(72)	Tumacacori	Arizona	*
(73)	Tuzigoot	Arizona	*
(74)	Walnut Canyon	Arizona	3
(75)	White Sands	New Mexico	229
(76)	Wupatki	Arizona	55

* indicates area less than one square mile; † newly established.

CANADA
UNITED STATES
MONTANA
NORTH DAKOTA
Missouri River
Williston
Minot
Mandan
Bismarck
Yellowstone River
Billings
GRANITE PEAK
Sheridan
Cody
Greybull
Yellowstone National Park
ROCKY
GRAND TETON
WYOMING
SOUTH DAKOTA
Deadwood
BLACK HILLS
Rapid City
Pierre
Badlands National Monument
MINNESOTA
Chadron
NEBRASKA
Casper
Missouri River
Yankton
Sioux Falls
Sioux City
IOWA
Dunlap
Rawlins
Scottsbluff
North Platte River
Green Sea of Dunes
Oshkosh
North Platte
Grand Island
Kearney
Omaha
Council Bluffs
Green River
MEDICINE BOW PEAK
Laramie
Cheyenne
Platte River
Lincoln
MOUNTAINS
City
Steamboat Springs
Greeley
South Platte River
Sterling
McCook
Pawnee City
St. Joseph
MISSOURI
gos Cave Monument
Fraser
Boulder
Denver
Burlington
Hill City
Leavenworth
Kansas City
Price
Greenwood Springs
SANGRE
Climax
Aspen
Leadville
MT. ELBERT
Buena Vista
PIKES PEAK
Colorado Springs
Goodland
Hays
Abilene
Salina
Topeka
Archess National Park
Grand Junction
COLORADO
Pueblo
KANSAS
Emporia
yonlands nal Park
Moab
DE CRISTO MTS
La Junta
Garden City
Hutchinson
Arkansas River
Wichita
al ea
UNCOMPAHGRE PEAK
Great Sand Dunes National Monument
Walsenburg
Dodge City
Monticello
Blanding
Durango
Alamosa
Trinidad
Boise City
Bartlesville
ke Powell
MOUNTAINS
Raton
Woodward
Enid
Claremore
Monument Valley
Farmington
WHEELER PEAK
Tulsa
Ship Rock
SAN JUAN BASIN
Taos
Canadian River
Muskogee
City
Canyon de Chelly National Monument
Los Alamos
Santa Fe
Las Vegas
OKLAHOMA
ERT
Crater Monument
Gallup
Albuquerque
Oklahoma City
Holbrook
Petrified Forest National Park
Amarillo
Lawton
Ardmore
NEW MEXICO
Red River
Wichita Falls
NA
Lubbock
Roswell
Pecos River
Fort Worth
Dallas
uaro nal Monument
Morenci
Alamogordo
White Sands National Monument
Silver City
Rio Grande
Carlsbad Caverns National Park
Carlsbad
Sweetwater
Brazos River
TEXAS
Deming
Las Cruces
Whites City
Midland
Waco
El Paso
San Angelo
ogales
Douglas
Tombstone
Austin

INDIANA
ILLINOIS
New Albany
Louisville
Frankfort
Lexington
Evansville
Ohio River
KENTUCKY
Danville
Cairo
Paducah
Bowling Green
Glasgow
Mammoth Cave National Park
Nashville
Oak Ridge
Knoxville
TENNESSEE

130°
130°
65°
60°
135°
Glacier Bay
Monument
Gustavus
Haines
Bellingham
North Cascades
National Park
Glacier
National Park
Port Angeles
Mt. Vernon
Kalispell
Olympic National Park
Bremerton
Seattle
Spokane
Coeur d'Alene
WASHINGTON
Great Falls
Long Beach
Olympia
Tacoma
MT. RAINIER
Missoula
Helena
Yakima
Richland
Lewiston
Anaconda
Butte
Astoria
Walla Walla
Pendleton
BITTERROOT RANGE
Vancouver
Columbia River
Portland
MT. HOOD
The Dalles
Virginia City
45°
Salem
Weiser
BORAH PEAK
CASCADE RANGE
OREGON
Ontario
IDAHO
Eugene
GREAT SANDY DESERT
Boise
Sun Valley
Arco
Crater Lake
National Park
Atomic City
COLUMBIA PLATEAU
Medford
Pocatello
Klamath Falls
Twin Falls
Lava Beds
National Monument
MT. SHASTA
Eureka
Winnemucca
Great Salt
Lake
Ogden
Redding
Elko
Salt Lake
MT. LASSEN
40°
Red Bluff
Timpanogos
National
Provo
Reno
GREAT BASIN
SACRAMENTO VALLEY
Truckee
Sacramento River
COAST RANGE
SIERRA NEVADA
Virginia City
Carson City
NEVADA
Lake Tahoe
Ely
UTAH
Petaluma
Sacramento
WASATCH RANGE
Stockton
Yosemite
National Park
Milford
Berkeley
Oakland
Tonopah
San Francisco
Bryce Canyon
National Park
Glen Canyon
Recreation Area
Santa Clara
Modesto
Zion
National Park
San Jose
Merced
BOUNDARY
PEAK
St. George
Kanab
CALIFORNIA
Kings Canyon
National Park
Coral Pink Sand
Dunes State Park
Page
Salinas
Fresno
MT. WHITNEY
Grand Canyon
National Monument
Monterey
Sequoia
National Park
PAINTED DESERT
Visalia
Death Valley
National Monument
Las Vegas
Grand Canyon
National Park
Lake Mead
Tuba
SAN JOAQUIN VALLEY
Colorado River
Boulder City
Lake Mead
National
Recreation Area
35°
Bakersfield
HUMPHREYS
PEAK
Sunset
National
Kingman
Santa Barbara
Flagstaff
Needles
MOJAVE DESERT
PACIFIC OCEAN
Burbank
Pasadena
Prescott
Los Angeles
Ontario
San Bernardino
ARIZONA
Long Beach
Palm Springs
Colorado River
Phoenix
SONORA
DESERT
Gila River
San Diego
El Centro
Calexico
Yuma
Ajo
Tucson
UNITED STATES
MEXICO
Colorado Delta
GULF OF
CALIFORNIA
120°
115°
120°
115°